The author's objective in this book is to trace, through the writings of Paul Tillich and related studies, Tillich's concepts of theonomy, autonomy, and heteronomy, and to examine their implicit and explicit implications for the pedagogical principles of Christian education.

Dr. Lo starts from the hypothesis that the concept of theonomy in Tillich's thought is intimately related to some of the most important ideas in his theology — e.g., autonomy and heteronomy, Ultimate Reality, the New Being, the Spiritual Presence, faith, reason, history, and culture. He also hypothesizes that Tillich's concept of theonomy is most compatible with the pedagogical principles of the reconstructed liberal group in Christian education; his concept of heteronomy with the pedagogical principles of the conservative group; and his concept of autonomy with those of the liberal group. Both hypotheses were proved affirmatively in the book.

Born in Taiwan and having received Japanese, Chinese, and British education there, the author came to the United States where he furthered his studies at Pasadena College, Boston, Harvard, and New York Universities. He is an ordained minister in the United Presbyterian Church in the U.S.A. and currently a professor of Non-Western Civilization at Seton Hall University in South Orange, New Jersey.

Tillichian Theology and
Educational Philosophy

Tillichian Theology
and
Educational Philosophy

by

SAMUEL E. LO

Seton Hall University
Department of Asian Studies

PHILOSOPHICAL LIBRARY
New York

Copyright, 1970, by PHILOSOPHICAL LIBRARY, INC.,
15 East 40 Street, New York, N. Y. 10016

Library of Congress Catalog Card No. 70-124516

SBN 8022-2029-0

MANUFACTURED IN THE UNITED STATES OF AMERICA

To

BETTY,

MY WIFE

WITH AND WITHOUT
WHOM . . .

CONTENTS

CHAPTER I

Introduction

It is the purpose of this chapter to state *The Problem, Specific Problems, Definition of Terms, Delimitations, Basic Assumption, Basic Hypotheses,* along with the presentation of *The Structure of the Thesis* and the *Procedure in Collecting and Treating Data.*

THE PROBLEM

GENERAL STATEMENT

The problem of this study was to trace, through his own writings and with reference also to the related literature, (1) Paul Tillich's concepts of theonomy, autonomy, and heteronomy and (2) their implicit and explicit implications for pedagogical principles of Christian education.

SPECIFIC PROBLEMS

The specific problems which were inherent in the basic problem are listed below:

1. To trace Paul Tillich's concept of theonomy through his own writings with reference also to the related literature on the same subject.
2. To explore Tillich's discourses on the ideas of autonomy and heteronomy in connection specifically with the concept of theonomy.
3. To establish a frame of reference pertaining to the pedagogical principles of Christian education.
4. To relate Tillich's teachings on the concepts of theonomy, autonomy, and heteronomy to the pedagogical principles of Christian education as established in the preceding subproblem.

1

DEFINITION OF TERMS

As used in this research, certain specific or technical terms are defined as follows:

1. *Theonomy:* The term theonomy is taken from two Greek words, θεος (theos—god),[1] and νομος (nomos—law); therefore, when it is literally translated, theonomy means the law of God. In this research, and in accordance with Tillich's usage of it, the term signifies where God's law abides; where God is present and rules; and where the individuals and community are "open to and directed toward the divine."[2] Or, again, in Tillich's own words, it is "the state of culture under the impact of the Spiritual Presence,"[3] "a culture in which the ultimate meaning of existence shines through all finite forms of thought and action."[4]

2. *Autonomy:* The term autonomy is derived from αυτος (autos—inner), and nomos (law). It means "obedience to reason,"[5] and maintains that "man is his own law"[6]; and is to rely upon and use man's power of reason to its utmost degree. It is the assertion of human beings as self-sufficient and self-reliable existents.

3. *Heteronomy:* As used in this research, the term heteronomy means—as the etymology reveals its roots, ἕτερος (heteros—strange) and nomos (law)—the situation in which an external law or rule imposes itself upon man. Tillich said heteronomy "imposes an alien law, religious or secular, on man's mind,"[7] and, therefore, is the deprivation or suppression of autonomous power, undermining "creative freedom and the humanity of man."[8]

4. *Implicit:* As used in this study, the term implicit means "fairly to be understood, but not specifically stated; implied," or "virtually contained in; essential, though not apparent."[9]

5. *Explicit:* Throughout this study, the term explicit means "plainly expressed," or "having no disguised meaning or reservation; definite; open; unreserved."[10]

---

[1] Note: This researcher follows Tillich's precedent in not underlining theos, nomos, autos, heteros, kairos, and certain other foreign words in this thesis.

[2] Paul Tillich, *The Protestant Era,* p. 44.

[3] ————, *Systematic Theology III,* p. 249.

[4] ————, *The Protestant Era,* Introduction, xii.

[5] *Ibid.,* p. 44.

[6] *Ibid.,* p. 56.

[7] *Ibid.,* p. 46.

[8] Tillich, *The Protestant Era,* p. 46.

[9] *New Standard Dictionary of the English Language,* p. 1235.

[10] *Ibid.,* p. 878.

2

6. *Pedagogical:* According to the *Webster's New International Dictionary,* the term pedagogical means that which is "concerned with, or treating of, pedagogics or education." It further defines pedagogics as the "science or art of teaching; principles and rules of teaching."[11] As used in this research, pedagogics, or its equivalent term, pedagogy, is "the theory or the teaching of how to teach."[12]

7. *Principle:* This term, according to *The Oxford English Dictionary,* signifies "that from which something takes its rise, originates, or is derived; a source; the root," or "an original or native tendency or faculty; a natural or innate disposition; a fundamental quality which constitutes the source of action."[13] Or, as the *Webster's Seventh New Collegiate Dictionary* puts it in a simpler way: Principle, it reads, is "a comprehensive and fundamental law, doctrine, or assumption."[14]

8. *Christian Education:* Paul H. Vieth, writing in *The Church and Christian Education* in 1947, says, "Christian education is the process by which persons are confronted with and controlled by the Christian gospel. It involves the efforts of the Christian community to guide both young and adult persons toward an ever richer possession of the Christian heritage and a fuller participation in the life and work of the Christian fellowship."[15]

9. *Conservative Christian educators:* Those who voluntarily impose upon themselves, or willingly accept, certain authority, law, or rule—be it the authority of the Bible, creed, articles of faith, or rule of conduct.[16]

10. *Liberal Christian educators:* Those who adhere to "the employment of the scientific method of inquiry," by subjecting any law, belief, authority, or experience to rational-empirical exploration and scientific verification. These liberals also claim that man is of infinite dignity and value as man.[17]

11. *Reconstructed Liberal Christian educators:* Those who stress both the revealed character of the Christian faith and the place of reason in determining the substance of Christian belief—in receiving, interpreting, and communicating revelation. They believe that the establishment of the Kingdom of God depends indeed on God himself but stress most

---

[11] *Webster's New International Dictionary,* p. 1589.
[12] *Standard Dictionary of the English Language,* p. 929.
[13] *The Oxford English Dictionary,* p. 1376.
[14] *Webster's Seventh New Collegiate Dictionary,* p. 676.
[15] Paul H. Vieth, *The Church and Christian Education,* p. 52.
[16] *The Westminster Dictionary of Christian Education,* p. 272.
[17] *Ibid.,* p. 390.

strongly at the same time that it also hinges on the faithful obedience of man in subjecting all human experience, interpersonal relationships, cultural creations, and social institutions to God's will.[18]

DELIMITATIONS

1. This study is delimited to Tillich's works appearing in English. In 1932 he was introduced to the English-speaking world by H. Richard Niebuhr's translation of *The Religious Situation* from the German text. *The Interpretation of History* was published in 1936 and consists of translations of seven essays published in German from 1924 to 1933 and an autobiographical sketch. These essays Tillich had previously considered his most important work not yet appearing in English. After 1936 Tillich wrote his major works exclusively in English for publication and asserted frequently that there was no need to go to German sources for an understanding of his thought.

2. The scope of this study is also delimited to Tillich's concept of theonomy and the ideas that have direct bearing on it.

3. This study is delimited to the theoretical implications of Tillich's theology for the pedagogical principles of Christian education.

4. Lastly, the analysis of the principles of Christian education is delimited to selected Christian educators who are clearly representative of the conservative, liberal, and reconstructed liberal groups within Christian education.[19]

BASIC ASSUMPTION

It is assumed that the English translations of Tillich's German writings are reasonable, faithful, and accurate reproductions of the original texts and that, therefore, they are to be treated as reliable, dependable, valid, and authoritative sources for the purpose of this study.

---

[18] *Ibid.*, p. 460.

[19] Note: It is acknowledged that a neat classification of categories according to theological persuasions is almost impossible. For instance, the first category adopted by this researcher, the "conservative group" is also known as the "fundamentalist group," or, more recently, the "evangelical group," or simply, the "orthodox." Likewise, the third category, the "reconstructed liberal group," is also termed the "neo-orthodox group," or the "neo-liberal group," or, more recently, the "neo-Reformation group."

Reference is made to the respective category or term in *The Westminster Dictionary of Christian Education*, edited by Kendig B. Cully, in 1963.

BASIC HYPOTHESES

1. It is hypothesized that the concept of theonomy in Tillich's thought is intimately related to some of the most important ideas in his theology—such ideas as autonomy and heteronomy.

2. It is also hypothesized that Tillich's concept of theonomy is most compatible with the pedagogical principles of the reconstructed liberal group in Christian education, his concept of heteronomy with the pedagogical principles of the conservative group, and his concept of autonomy with those of the liberal group.

THE STRUCTURE OF THE THESIS

Immediately following this Introduction, the second chapter is devoted to the presentation of the life, work, and the significance of Paul Tillich. The third chapter deals wholly with the central concept in this thesis, which is Tillich's concept of theonomy. The next chapter treats two ideas which have direct bearings on the concept of theonomy. They are: the concepts of autonomy and heteronomy in Tillich's theological system. The pedagogical principles under three distinctive groups —namely, the conservative, the liberal, and the reconstructed liberal groups—in Protestant Christian education are treated in the fifth and sixth chapters. The seventh and final chapter is comprised of Summary and Conclusion in which the implications of the concepts of theonomy, autonomy, and heteronomy in Tillich's theology for the pedagogical principles as found in the preceding two chapters are drawn. This chapter is followed by the Bibliography.

PROCEDURE IN COLLECTING AND TREATING DATA

What is intended in the concluding paragraphs of this chapter is to make explicit what has been done in regard to the collecting and treating of the data for this research.[20]

In November, 1963, this researcher started to concentrate on rereading Tillich's books while simultaneously he launched into a search for other writings by Tillich—as well as for commentaries on Tillich's work and thought. This undertaking reached through the mails as far as six foreign countries—West Pakistan, Switzerland, Scotland, England,

---

[20] Note: Anyone who is interested in the detailed Procedure in Collecting and Treating Data is referred to the corresponding sections in this investigator's Research Design, pp. 23-42.

Canada, and Japan—and scores of different places in the United States. Altogether the writer collected over one hundred and fifty items by or on Tillich, and since he was privileged to borrow, in person or through mail, books and articles from the libraries of Union Theological Seminary in New York, Princeton Theological Seminary in Princeton, New Jersey, and Harvard University Divinity School in Cambridge, Massachusetts, he was able to have access to over two hundred items on Tillich.

Employing the same methodology, by early 1966 he had collected, or borrowed, whenever the desired volumes were out of print, the books on Christian education that were needed for the writings of this thesis.

During and after the undertaking mentioned above, this researcher read and reread the sources for the purpose of (1) grasping Tillich's theological system as a whole and (2) getting intimately acquainted with the pedagogical principles of Christian education by reading the major books in the field. Then he collected and arranged the data needed for the solution of the subproblems. The paragraphs, sentences, or phrases relevant to the concepts to be dealt with, and the problems to be solved, were drawn from the sources listed in the Bibliography at the end of the thesis. Dozens of questions pertaining to these concepts and pedagogical principles were put to the sources in order to secure the data needed for the solution of each subproblem.

CHAPTER II

Life, Work, and Significance

The first part of this chapter is concerned with the life and work of Paul Tillich and the second part with his significance as a theological thinker.

I. LIFE AND WORK

It is difficult to appreciate the thought of a leading thinker if one is totally unacquainted with his life. This is the justification for this section, in spite of the fact that there are three autobiographical sketches by the subject himself and that numerous authors have devoted their first chapters to this purpose.[1] What is intended in this part then is a brief introduction to Tillich's life in conjunction with some of his work, reserving his significance as a man to the second half of this chapter.

Paul Tillich was born on the 20th of August, 1886, in a village manse in Starzeddel, near Guben, a small industrial town in the province of Brandenburg, at the Silesian border, where his father was a minister of the Prussian Territorial Church. Four years later the family moved to Schönfliess-Neumark because his father was called to the position of superintendent of a group of Lutheran parishes in the diocese. It was a place of three thousand inhabitants and from his fourth to

---

[1] See *The Interpretation of History*, 1936; *The Protestant Era*, 1948; Kegley and Bretall. (ed.), *The Theology of Paul Tillich*, 1952. Also Walter Leibrecht, (ed.), *Religion and Culture: Essays in Honor of Paul Tillich*, 1959, "The Life and Mind of Paul Tillich," pp. 3-27; George H. Tavard, *Paul Tillich and the Christian Message*, 1962, "The Mind of Paul Tillich," pp. 1-14; J. Heywood Thomas, *Paul Tillich: An Appraisal*, 1963, "Life and Development," pp. 11-19; and Bernard Martin, *The Existentialist Theology of Paul Tillich*, 1963, "The Life of Paul Tillich," pp. 15-26, etc.

twelfth year the young Paul Tillich lived in this walled medieval town, built around an old Gothic church and surrounded by historical landmarks. The boy was sent to the common school at first, but after receiving private lessons in Latin he later went to a humanistic gymnasium in Königsberg-Neumark, a somewhat larger medieval town than Schönfliess and not too far from it. These medieval towns in which he spent the first fourteen years of his life made an ineradicable impression on his mind, as did the nature and country life with which he was surrounded. Nearly all his great memories and strong longings are linked with the soil, weather, wind, and woods. However, it was also during these years that he made frequent visits to Berlin, his father's birthplace; and these visits were for him a source of excitement as well as of mysterious feeling as for any child brought up in the country when he sees a big city and its life.

He was overjoyed, therefore, when his father was called to an important church post in Berlin in 1900 and the family moved to the capital. In Old Berlin he again enrolled in a humanistic gymnasium, passed his final examinations, and was graduated in 1904. The basic subjects in the curriculum of the gymnasium were Greek and Latin, and it was here that he cultivated a lifelong love for the Greek language through which he came to appreciate the Greek culture and especially the early Greek philosophers. He also acquired a good foundation in the history of philosophy and a basic acquaintance with Fichte and Kant, and later with Schleiermacher, Hegel, and Schelling. In 1904 he was matriculated in the theological faculties of the universities of Berlin, Tübingen, and Halle. In 1909 he took his first and in 1911 his second theological examination and received the degree of Doctor of Philosophy in Breslau in the latter year. A year later he was awarded the degree of Licentiate of Theology in Halle and in the same year was ordained in the Evangelical Lutheran Church of the province of Brandenburg.

Before leaving his student years, it might be helpful to get a glimpse of the personalities of his parents from whom he gained certain insights important for his theological development in the future. Both his father and mother were strong personalities, but of contrasting types and representing divergent Germanic traditions and temperaments.

> My father was a conscientious, very dignified, completely convinced and in the presence of doubt, angry supporter of the conservative Lutheran point of view. My mother, coming from the more democratic and liberal Rhineland, did not have the authori-

tarian attitude. She was, however, deeply influenced by the rigid morals of Western Reformed Protestantism. The consequence was a restrictive pressure in thought as well as in action, in spite (and partly because) of a warm atmosphere of loving care. Every attempt to break through was prevented by the unavoidable guilt consciousness produced by the identification of the parental with the divine authority.[2]

However, "by using the very principles established by (his) father's authoritarian system" he was finally able to free himself from this parental bondage through long philosophical discussions which were at the same time to become the most happy instances of a positive relation to his father. It is, nevertheless, attributable to this difficult and painful break-through to autonomy that he was made immune to any system of thought or life which demanded a surrender of this autonomy.

Following the termination of his theological studies, Tillich served for two years as assistant pastor of various parishes of the Old Prussian United Church, but when the First World War broke out he immediately volunteered as a chaplain and served with the German army from September 1914 to September 1918. It was during this period that a drastic change occurred in his thinking. He experienced overwhelmingly for the first time an awareness of a nation-wide community; heretofore he had been concerned with a merely individualistic and purely theoretical existence. Then came the realization that the unity of his nation was a myth, that Germany was divided into conflicting classes, and that the proletarian masses considered the church to be unquestionably an ally of their enemies, the ruling classes. It took him only a few months to lose all his enthusiasm for his nation's war adventures and to become convinced that the war would not end until the ruination of all of Europe had been completed. His sympathy rested increasingly with the oppressed and abused masses, and he unhesitatingly plunged himself into the movements for social change immediately after his discharge from the Army. He became a leader in the movement of Religious Socialism in the post-war years.

From 1919 to 1924 Tillich served as a Privatdozent of theology at the University of Berlin, where he lectured on subjects concerned with the relation of religion to politics, art, philosophy, depth psychology, and sociology. It was actually a "Theology of Culture,"—the title of a book that appeared some thirty-five years later—upon which he lectured. In 1924 Karl Becker, Tillich's friendly adviser and the minister

[2] Kegley and Bretall, ed., Ibid., p. 8.

of education persuaded him, though somewhat against his will, into a theological professorship in Marburg. Here Tillich encountered Heidegger and his existentialist doctrine of man. Here also he began work on his Systematic Theology, the first volume of which appeared in America twenty-six years later and the last volume in 1963. During a period of eight years, from 1925 to 1933, he taught as a professor of religion and social philosophy at Dresden, as a professor of theology at Leipzig, and, from 1929 until 1933, as a professor of philosophy at the University of Frankfurt.

Tillich's growing reputation as a scholar in German university circles, his many books and articles, and his frequent public lectures and speeches soon established him as one of the most important academic figures in Germany. Therefore, it was quite understandable that as soon as he opposed openly and passionately the newly-arising National Socialist movement he was marked as a dangerous man to Nazism. Upon the accession of Hitler to the German chancellorship in 1933, Tillich was immediately dismissed from his professorship at Frankfurt. Through an already accepted invitation and sponsorship of the Niebuhr brothers, Reinhold and the late Richard, he and his family arrived in New York on November 4, 1933.

For twenty-two years Tillich held the chair of professor of philosophical theology at Union Theological Seminary in New York, and upon his retirement from that institution he was invited to the distinguished position of a "University Professor" at Harvard University where he taught from 1955 to 1962. From the autumn of the latter year until his death on October 22, 1965, he was a professor of theology at the University of Chicago Divinity School.

Starting with the publication of the English translation of *The Religious Situation* from the German text, by H. Richard Niebuhr in 1932, Tillich produced an additional nineteen volumes, two of which were posthumous and three of which were books of sermons. The titles can be found in the Bibliography. He also wrote and had published over three hundred magazine articles, both in English and in German.

II. SIGNIFICANCE

Tillich has been widely acclaimed as one of the few unquestionably great men of the present generation, or as one of the foremost philosophers and most distinguished theologians in America.[3] When the edi-

---

[3] Kegley and Bretall, ed., *Ibid.*, p. 161.

tors of *The Library of Living Theology*, Professors Charles W. Kegley, of Wagner College, New York, and Robert W. Bretall, of the University of Arizona, conceived the idea of introducing the most influential theologians in this country, they did not hesitate at all in their choice of Tillich as the first man about whom to write a book. The editors were of the opinion that they were fully justified in their choice of Tillich for the first volume because of the depth, comprehensiveness, systematic structure, imaginativeness, and applicability of his thought. Following the scheme of Professor Paul A. Schilpp, of Northwestern University, in *The Library of Living Philosophers*, the book contains, beside "Autobiographical Reflections of Paul Tillich," "Reply to Interpretation and Criticism by Paul Tillich," and "Bibliography of the Writings of Paul Tillich to March, 1952," fourteen essays from prominent thinkers in the faculties of theology, philosophy, political science, and the social sciences in the institutions of higher learning in the United States and Europe. They are, to mention a few, Theodore M. Greene, of the Department of Philosophy, Yale University; Theodor Siegfried, of the Department of Theology, the University of Marburg, Germany; John H. Randell, Jr., of the Philosophy Department, Columbia University; Charles Hartshorne, of the Department of Philosophy, The University of Chicago; Reinhold Niebuhr, of Union Theological Seminary; Nels F. S. Ferré, of the Department of Religion, Vanderbilt University; and Edward Heimann, of the Graduate Faculty of Political and Social Science, New School for Social Research, New York City. These scholars were asked to take respective parts of Tillich's theology, by which his thought could be analyzed in a coherent way. Writing on "Tillich's Role in Contemporary Theology" in the same volume Walter M. Horton, of the Department of Philosophy of Christianity, The Graduate School of Theology, Oberlin College, made a survey of Tillich's influence on contemporary theology and discovered it to be extensively far-reaching—with impacts on (1) Continental Protestant theology, (2) American Protestant theology, (3) Catholic theology; and with implications for (a) a theology for the ecumenical movement, and (b) a theology for cultural reconstruction. Other contributions range from "The Method and Structure of Paul Tillich," "Tillich's Doctrine of Man," "The Ontology of Paul Tillich," "Tillich's Doctrine of God," to "Christology and Biblical Criticism in Tillich," and "Tillich's Interpretation of History." The editors themselves have this to say of him:

With Dewey, Whitehead, Russell and Santayana stands a man whom future generations probably will pronounce no whit their inferior either dialectically or in his grasp of the philosophical requirements of our time, but whose feet are planted solidly upon Christian soil, rooted in the Word of God. His name is Paul Tillich.[4]

There has been an increasing number of volumes[5] written on Tillich's system as a whole or on aspects of it and although their findings contain positive as well as negative conclusions, mixed with high praise and severe criticism, affirmations and denunciations, they prove that he is a truly controvertial and influential figure. J. Heywood Thomas, Head of the Department of Philosophy of Religion at the University of Manchester, England, since 1957, who had studied under Tillich at Union Theological Seminary in 1952 and whose purpose, among others, in his book, *Paul Tillich: An Appraisal*, was "to repay a pupil's double debt—to say what I have learned and to pull my teacher's work to bits," states that, "Nowadays it is widely recognized that he occupies a unique place in American theology, and it is not unjust to describe a great part of American theology as a commentary on his work."[6] Alexander J. McKelway, a brilliant young scholar on Tillichian and modern theologies, who taught at Dartmouth College and now teaches at Davidson College in South Carolina, wrote the following in 1964:

> In 1923 Karl Ludwig Schmidt wrote that "the discussion and commutation of systematic theology in our time will be in great measure determined on the one side by Barth and Gogarten, and on the other side by Tillich." These words have proven prophetic, for certainly today Paul Tillich represents one of the two or three most distinct and important directions of contemporary theology.[7]

Aside from these authors there have been in recent years a great many articles on Tillich[8] which testify to his pinnacled position among the Protestant system-builders.

[4] *Ibid.*, Introduction, x.

[5] See the first footnote in this chapter, on page 7. Also Kenneth Hamilton, The *System and the Gospel*, 1963; Alexander J. McKelway, *The Systematic Theology of Paul Tillich*, 1964; James L. Adams, *Paul Tillich's Philosophy of Culture, Science, and Religion*, 1965.

[6] Thomas, *op. cit.*, p. 19.

[7] McKelway, *op. cit.*, p. 19.

[8] John E. Skinner, "A Critique of Tillich's Ontology," American Theological Review, 1957, pp. 53-61; Will Herberg, *Four Existentialist Theologians*, 1958; "A Theology for Protestants," *Time*, March 16, 1959, pp. 46-52; Howard E. Hunter, "Tillich and Tennant: Two Types of Philosophical Theology," *Crane Review*, Spring, 1959, pp. 100-110; William H. Johnson, "Tillich's Science of Being," The *Princeton Seminary Bulletin*, October, 1962, pp. 52-62, et. al.

There have been over thirty doctoral dissertations written on Tillich, or still in progress, in American universities and divinity schools[9] and his theology has increasingly been referred to and studied by professors and students alike in the theological seminaries in this country.[10] In fact, his writings are being assigned to both graduate and undergraduate students in religion, philosophy, sociology, psychology, political science, and art more and more often, as his influence reaches further and wider among all fields of human pursuits upon which his thought has touched. His is a comprehensive thought system that encompasses all the fields of study mentioned above and some other spheres of human life in this intricately complex and utterly perplexing modern age. Being a prophetic voice since the 1930s, his urgent utterances and unparalleled emphases on man's necessity for being ultimately concerned with the ground of being and the meaning of life have been universally hailed as truly awakening and refreshing by those who are seeking answers, the questions of which have arisen out of the estranged, warring, and seemingly purposeless world in which man finds himself.

As a man whose starting point was always existential, Tillich endeavored tirelessly from this perspective to pull together through his method of correlation the centuries-long problems of the harmony and unity between theology and philosophy, religion and culture, church and the world, sacred and secular, symbols and art, and God and man. He also ceaselessly warned against the self-complacency and the sterilization of Protestantism and tried to revive its principle which will continue in service to God even after the Protestant era is to pass away.[11]

---

[9] Stephen Crary, "Idealistic Elements in Tillich's Thought," Yale University, 1955; Doi Masatoshi, "Paul Tillich's Eschatology and Its Social Implications," Hartford Seminary Foundation, 1955; Harold A. Jackson, "The Significance of Paul Tillich's Theology for a Philosophy of Religious Education," Stanford University, 1956; Eugene E. Wood, Jr., "Psychology of Personality in the Thought of Paul Tillich," Boston University, 1955; Thomas Langford, "A Critical Analysis of Paul Tillich's 'Method of Correlation'," Duke University, 1958; Donald Loutzenhiser, "Faith and Ultimate Concern: St. Paul and Paul Tillich," University of Southern California, 1960; Choan-seng Song, "The Relation of Divine Revelation and Man's Religion in the Theologies of Karl Barth and Paul Tillich," Union Theological Seminary, New York, 1964, et. al.

[10] The Bulletins of Vanderbilt University Divinity School, 1959-1960; Fuller Theological Seminary and San Francisco Theological Seminary, 1961-1962; The Pacific School of Religion, Pittsburgh Theological Seminary, Southern Methodist University, Southwestern Baptist Theological Seminary, and Westminster Theological Seminary, 1962-1963; Boston University School of Theology, Princeton Theological Seminary, and Union Theological Seminary, New York, 1963-1964; Harvard University Divinity School and Yale University Divinity School, 1964-1965, etc.

[11] The Protestant Era, pp. 185-233.

Not alone to the Protestants, Tillich's thought appeals to Roman Catholic theologians as well. This is evidenced by the fact that, aside from a recent book, over half a dozen articles on Tillich have appeared in Roman Catholic journals in the past decade or two,[12] and the Roman Catholic interest in his theology increases as years go by.

[12] George H. Tavard, *Paul Tillich and the Christian Message*, 1962.
Articles: Gustave Weigel, S. J., "Contemporaneous Protestantism and Paul Tillich," *Theological Studies*, Baltimore, 1950, pp. 177-202; also "The Theological Significance of Paul Tillich," *Cross Currents*, Winter, 1956, pp. 141-155; Avery R. Dules, S. J., "Paul Tillich and the Bible," *Theological Studies*, Baltimore, 1956, pp. 345-369; Kenelm Foster, O. P., "Paul Tillich and St. Thomas," *Blackfriars*, 1960, pp. 306-313; George H. Tavard, "Paul Tillich's System: When 'Protestant Principle' encounters 'Catholic Substance'," *Commonweal*, February 7, 1964, pp. 566-568; Duane R. Thompson, "Tillich's Esthetic of Ultimate Meaning," *Continuum*, Spring, 1965, pp. 68-74; Celestin D. Weisser, "Paul Tillich: A Roman Catholic Appreciation," *Christian Advocate*, February 10, 1966, pp. 7-8; George H. Tavard, "Tillich: Christ as the Answer to Existential Analysis," *Continuum*, Spring, 1966, pp. 3-12, etc.

CHAPTER III

Tillich's Concept of Theonomy

The purpose of this chapter is to trace Paul Tillich's concept of theonomy through his writings since 1932, when he was first introduced to the English-speaking world by the late H. Richard Niebuhr's English translation of *The Religious Situation* from the German text.

The materials used in connection with this part of the investigation are drawn exclusively from Tillich's own writings since the year 1932 and the writings of certain established scholars on Tillich's thought in recent years.

It must be granted at the outset that the concept of theonomy in Tillich's thought cannot be understood apart from the whole content of his theology and philosophy.[1] The scope of this chapter is confined, therefore, to the clarification of the exact meanings of the concept of theonomy *per se* in Tillich's theological system.

Determined by the content of data chosen for use, and for clarity's sake, this researcher has divided the present chapter into the following four sections: I. Theonomy in Tillich's Thought. II. Various Manifestations of Life in a Theonomous Encounter. III. Theonomy and History. IV. Theonomy and the Demonic.

I. THEONOMY IN TILLICH'S THOUGHT

This section is further divided into the following subsections: A. The meaning and characteristics of theonomy. B. God, Spiritual Presence, and theonomy. C. Faith and its consequences in theonomy.

---

[1] *Systematic Theology I*, vii and p. 184. Also Kegley and Bretall, ed., *op. cit.*, pp. 86 and 262; Hamilton, *op. cit.*, p. 14; and Adams, *op. cit.*, p. 18.

A. The Meaning and Characteristics of Theonomy

The difficulty some authors encountered[2] in Tillich's thought is instantaneously manifest as soon as one tries to define what Tillich meant by certain terms or definitions, such as theonomy, religion, or culture. However, the meaning of this term, theonomy, can be detected from the characteristics, or qualities, that were attributed by Tillich himself to this concept.

He stated that theonomy communicates "the experience of the holiness, of something ultimate in being and meaning in all its creations." Theonomy affirms "the autonomous forms of creative process," yet at the same time it is engaged in the "permanent struggle against both an independent heteronomy and an independent autonomy."[3] It is the transcendent foundation which gives both autonomy and heteronomy depth, unity, and ultimate meaning. Although Tillich was identified with various schools of thought, such as Naturalism, Pantheism, Supernaturalism, Idealism, or Existentialism, he declared succinctly that he would prefer to be identified as the man who invented and held the position of Belief-ful Realism, by which he meant "an attitude in which the reference to the transcendent and eternal source of meaning and ground of being is present."[4] It is, furthermore, the "unconditioned acceptance of the serious importance of our concrete situation in time and of the situation of time in general in the presence of eternity." Its goal is "the free devotion of finite forms to the eternal."[5]

The most precise statement of theonomy found in Tillich is: "Religion is the substance of culture and culture the form of religion." In the same book, *The Protestant Era*, he wrote, "Theonomy has been defined as a culture in which the ultimate meaning of existence shines through all finite forms of thoughts and action; the culture is transparent, and its creations are vessels of a spiritual content." It is, in other words, a state in which "everything relative becomes the vehicle of the absolute and the insight that nothing relative can ever become absolute itself."[6]

Another characteristic which Tillich attached to the idea of theonomy is the wholeness and centeredness of a person, a culture, or a

[2] Nels F. S. Ferré, "Tillich's View of the Church," *The Theology of Paul Tillich*, pp. 248ff; and Hamilton, *Ibid.*, pp. 17f; etc.
[3] *ST III*, p. 251.
[4] *The Religious Situation*, p. 12.
[5] *Ibid.*, pp. 116 and 216, respectively.
[6] *The Protestant Era*, pp. 57, Introduction xii, and 47, respectively.

period under its impact. He enunciated, "where there is theonomy nothing which is considered true and just is sacrificed. Theonomous periods do not feel split, but whole and centered."[7] The concept of 'wholeness' in Tillich is, incidentally, equivalent to the ideas of salvation and healing,[8] which shows the close correlation between the theonomous state and salvation, or being made whole and integrated as a person, a society, or an age.

Semantically speaking, the term, theonomy, is comprised of two Greek words: θεος (God), and νομος (law). The idea of God in Tillich is expanded briefly in the next subsection. Nomos, according to *A Pocket Lexicon to the Greek New Testament*, can sometimes be interpreted as "the body of moral and ceremonial enactments, or a power to legislate, a sense of law, something with legislative authority . . . an ordinance, as found in Romans 7: 2."[9] It would be gravely erroneous, however, if one tries to interpret theonomy as the law of God which is imposed upon men from the supernatural sphere. So interpreted, theonomy would be nothing but heteronomy. Tillich himself stated explicitly: Theonomy does not mean the divine law, for if it means only this, it has the same meaning as heteronomy. Theonomy means rather that the forms of autonomy point beyond themselves, without being destroyed or interfered with on their own ground, to the ground from which they come, and which they reflect and form and shape. It (the voice or power from another dimension) elevates a situation into the light of a new dimension, the dimension of that which is ultimately important and infinitely significant, "elevating a piece out of the ordinary context of temporal things and events, making it translucent for the Divine glory." It is furthermore, "a state of mind and reality in which the divine is manifested."[10] It is a state in which all the cultural forms and their autonomous creation, in art, in music, in sciences, in politics, in morals, in social relations, everywhere, all these forms have one point which has the line of the vertical.

It may be concluded that in theonomy some ultimate meaning is expressed in all of the cultural activities and creations and that some-

---

[7] *ST I*, p. 148.

[8] *The New Being*, pp. 34f; and "Baccalaureate Address: Salvation," *The Princeton Seminary Bulletin*, October, 1963, pp. 4-9.

[9] Alexander Souter, *A Pocket Lexicon to the Greek New Testament*. Oxford: Oxford University Press, 1948, p. 167.

[10] "Christian Criteria for Our Culture," *Criterion*, October, 1952, p. 3; *The New Being*, pp. 116 and 120; and "The Basic Ideas of Religious Socialism," *The Bulletin*, The International House of Japan, Inc., October, 1960, p. 14, respectively.

thing ultimate, infinite, and eternal has happened in history; in the forms of the daily life of all the cultural production; and that an answer to the questions of every human being, hidden or open, is given with the transforming power to guide and direct the finite to the infinite, weaving into itself a touch of the divine in the process. In the concluding paragraph of the Author's Preface in his book, *The Religious Situation*, Tillich disclosed that "if the book succeeds in bearing effective testimony to the shaking . . . of our time by eternity it will have fulfilled its purpose."[11] The Protestant principle—not Protestantism nor the Protestant church—embraces such a theonomous element since it is to protest "in the name of absoluteness of the absolute, the ultimateness of the ultimate denying any finite which claims ultimacy."[12]

B. God, Spiritual Presence, and Theonomy

It is by no means this researcher's intention to make a complete analysis of Tillich's ideas of God. Such an undertaking would undoubtedly call for another doctoral dissertation. It is in accord with this researcher's scheme, however, to introduce a few basic ideas in Tillich's doctrine of God that have direct bearings on the concept of theonomy at this stage of the investigation. Tillich himself acknowledged that "the idea of God is the foundation of every theological thought," and that over against Supernaturalism and Naturalism, his way of interpreting the doctrine of God is "self-transcendent," or "ecstatic": it goes beyond itself in order to return to itself in a new dimension. In the same volume, he wrote that God "is the infinite, or the unconditional, or being-itself . . . in the sense of the power of being or the power to conquer non-being."[13] To him, God is, first of all, being as such. Then, it is the power of being in everything that participates in the being. In a theonomous situation every finite reality is rooted in the creative ground of being itself. Speaking to a Jewish as well as Protestant and Catholic

---

[11] *The Religious Situation*, p. 27.

Note: In the same book Tillich stated on page 217 that Barthian dialectical theology, with its prophetic and penetrative document, *Commentary on the Epistle to the Romans*, "lets the judgment of the unconditionedly transcendent God fall upon every attempt of culture or religion to claim value before him. In its conception the only relation which the world has to God is that the world stands in the divine negation, in the crisis, in the shaking of time by eternity."

[12] "The Protestant Vision," *The Chicago Theological Seminary Register*, March, 1950, p. 11.

[13] *ST II*, pp. 5-11.

audience at the Park Avenue Synagogue in early 1953, Tillich made this statement:

> I speak of God who is the creative ground of everything, who is always present, always creating and destroying, always experienced as nearer to ourselves than we ourselves are, always unapproachable, holy, fascinating, terrifying, the ground and meaning of everything that is. This is the living God, dynamic in himself, life as the ground of life. . . .[14]

"We may be able to hurl Him out of our consciousness, to reject Him, to refute Him, to argue convincingly for His non-existence, and to live very comfortably without Him," but "He is God only because He is inescapable. And only that which is inescapable is God."[15] It is what the Psalmist says, "If I ascend up into heaven, thou art there: if I make my bed in hell, behold, thou art there."[16] As God is omnipresent, so is his Spirit and his Kingdom. And wherever the divine Spirit is present, there theonomy will be established fragmentarily— fragmentarily because there can be no complete or perfect theonomy in human existence. A complete theonomy can come about only in the fullness of the Kingdom of God,[17] where complete transparency of everything makes it possible for the divine to shine through it. At a theonomous moment, the Spiritual Presence speaks to individuals, groups, and institutions, "grasping them, inspiring them, and transforming them."[18]

Elsewhere,[19] Tillich equated theonomy to culture as a whole under the impact of the Spiritual Presence. The term is used for "the state of culture under the impact of the Spiritual Presence. The nomos (law) effective in it is the directness of the self-creation of life under the dimension of the Spirit toward the ultimate in being and meaning." Speaking of the quest for a new theonomy arising from the permanent struggle between autonomous independence and heteronomous reaction, both in particular situations and in the depth of the cultural conscious-

---

[14] "Jewish Influences on Contemporary Christian Theology," *Cross Currents*, 1953, p. 40.

[15] *The Shaking of the Foundations*, pp. 41 and 40, respectively.

Note: All the Biblical passages in this thesis are taken from the King James Version, except the quotations from the sources used.

[16] Psalm 139: 8.

[17] *ST I*, p. 54.

[18] *The Eternal Now*, p. 84.

[19] *ST III*, p. 249.

ness in general, Tillich summarized the relationship between the Spiritual Presence and theonomy as follows:

> This quest is answered by the impact of the Spiritual Presence on culture. Wherever this impact is effective, theonomy is created, and wherever there is theonomy, traces of the impact of the Spiritual Presence are visible.[20]

C. Faith and Its Consequences in Theonomy

Religion is concerned with the relation of man to the eternal. In theonomy, it is God who, through his revelation and the impact of the Spiritual Presence, takes the initiative in establishing the dialogue, the relation, and the covenant. All that remains in this relation is for man to respond, to answer, and to proceed from the temporal and human. Although more discussions on the nature, place, and function of faith will be made sporadically throughout this investigation, suffice it to say at this juncture that in every theonomous situation there is required a voluntary and affirmative step to be taken by man. The state of mind in faith is best described by Tillich's emphasis on ultimate concern, which is at the central core of a religion, or of a theonomous state. Within the concept of ultimate concern is implied the concepts of ultimate seriousness, ultimate devotion, ultimate judgment, and ultimate expectation.[21] It is the great commandment expressed unambiguously and forcefully in Deuteronomy chapter 6, verse 5: Thou shalt love the Lord thy God with all thine heart, and with all thy soul, and with all thy might. Therein is embodied a genuine and complete response to the demand of total surrender to the subject of ultimate concern. Faith, to Tillich, is the state of being grasped by the Spiritual Presence and opened to the transcendent unity of unambiguous life. In Tillichian expression, faith is the state of being grasped and simultaneously transformed by the power of the New Being as it is manifested in Jesus of Nazareth as the Christ, the logos from God. It is a state in which the conditioned surrenders itself to become a vehicle for the unconditional without ceasing to be a conditioned. When this occurs, "there is an acceptance of the eternal manifesting itself in a special moment of history . . . (an) openness to the unconditional."[22]

When genuine faith meets head-on with God's self-revelation, it

---

[20] *Ibid.*, p. 252.
[21] "Christian Criteria for Our Culture," *Criterion*, October, 1952, p. 1.
[22] *The Protestant Era*, p. 43.

is inevitable that certain resulting consequences or effects will ensue. A new dimension will be opened toward the possessor of that faith; and so will the depth and meaning of life, event, and history. He will have a glimpse of the fathomless ground of his own being, and through this will be reunited with himself, with others, and with the ground of all being; and thereby, he will have the spiritual substance of his life preserved, protected, and recharged.[23] Another consequence of divine-human encounter is, as was stated in a previous section, man's new reception of answers to the questions which arise from the human existence, or more specifically from the predicaments and puzzlements in life. Tillich stated that theonomy, as the creation of the Spiritual Presence in the human situation, gives answers. In and through these answers, something of the inexhaustible depth of life becomes manifest. It is the state of blessedness in which fulfillment in the ultimate dimension of man's being is realized.[24] The new reality which is created through the Spiritual Presence in New Being at a theonomous moment does not remove the old beings, however, but transforms them into a new estate for divine purposes.

In the concluding paragraph of his sermon, "Spiritual Presence," in *The Eternal Now*, Tillich summarized beautifully and succinctly the fruits of I-Thou encounter:

> I could say that the work of the Spirit, liberating us from the law, is freedom. Or I could say that its work is faith, or that its work is hope, and above all, that the Spirit creates love, the love in which all laws are confirmed and fulfilled and at the same time overcome. . . . We know that it is great and holy, deep and abundant, ecstatic and sober, limited and distorted by time, fulfilled by eternity . . . in whom (Christ) the Spirit and the life are manifest without limits.[25]

II. VARIOUS MANIFESTATIONS OF LIFE IN A THEONOMOUS ENCOUNTER

Religion, in Tillich's thought, is two-faced: in its narrower sense religion is the organized religious bodies as peoples have them around the world—Islam, Christianity, Buddhism, Hinduism and the others. In its broad sense, however, it becomes more inclusive: Religion in this sense embraces also the quasi-religions, or so-called pseudo-religions,

---

[23] See Tavard, *op. cit.*, p. 117; also *The New Being*, p. 13, and *ST III*, p. 274.
[24] *ST III*, p. 253.
[25] *The Eternal Now*, p. 90f.

among which Communism, Humanism, Socialism, and Democracy are all included.[26] Tillich interpreted all these secular "isms" as the distorted manifestation of a religious concern. Interpreted in this frame of reference, it means that all human beings are religious no matter what social, political or religious forms their experiences may ultimately take as organized human expressions. To him who is arrested by God—or within the context of this thesis it may as well be said that to him who is in a theonomous situation—the transcendence over religion and non-religion, or irreligion, is achieved; and if he holds fast to the religious body to which he belongs its significance to him becomes drastically different. It becomes a channel and nothing but a channel through which the eternal is come to him. By achieving freedom from religion, he also has reached freedom for religion, making it alive and meaning-bestowing. He is blessed in it and he can be blessed outside of it, because he has been opened to the ultimate dimension of being-in-itself. In fact Tillich was of the opinion that the Spiritual Presence is not bound in any way to the religious realm but can even be effective through outspoken foes of religion, including Christianity.[27]

There are two spheres, according to Tillich, which can most outstandingly be pointed out as dimensions of life in and through which the substance of theonomous encounters reflects itself. They are: A. Church and Spiritual Community as Possessor of the New Being in Jesus Christ, and B. Culture.

A. CHURCH AND SPIRITUAL COMMUNITY AS POSSESSOR OF THE NEW BEING IN JESUS CHRIST

What is hoped to be accomplished in this subsection is to focus attention on the interrelationships between the church, as a spiritual community, and the New Being in Christ, a perfect embodiment and example of theonomous being.

Writing in *Systematic Theology III*, under the subtitle, "The Spiritual Presence and the New Being in the Spiritual Community,"[28] Tillich in brief tried to drive home the point that the New Being could not have brought the new reality without those who are willing to extend their acceptance of him. The dynamics of the Spiritual Presence in mankind must be seen in the following threefold sense: first, in mankind as a whole in preparation for the central manifestation of the di-

---

[26] *Christianity and the Encounter of the World Religions*, Chapter I.
[27] *The Eternal Now*, p. 111. See also *ST III*, p. 260.
[28] *ST III*, pp. 149-161.

vine Spirit; second, in the divine Spirit's basic manifestation of itself; and third, in the emergence of the holy community under the theonomous impact of the central event. In sum, it is the anticipation, the actual manifestation, and the reception of the appearance of the New Being in Jesus Christ. The church is the spiritual community in its receptive stage. The factuality of the reception is seen in the Christian doctrine of the church that regards itself as the embodiment of the New Being and the creation of the Spiritual Presence with its essential power in the spiritual community. The establishment of the Christian church is based on the claim that the revelation in Jesus as the Christ and as the perfect embodiment of the New Being is the final revelation; and, therefore, where this claim is absent, Christianity, along with the Christian church, ceases to exist. This statement implies that the Christ is not the Christ without the church and the church is not the church without Christ as its headstone.

Tillich elaborated further on this point[29] by stating that the church is the community of the New Being, and that the church, as the social and historical embodiment of the New Being, is not exactly an organized religion, and even less a hierarchical authority; neither is it merely a social organization, although it is all of these. It is primarily a group of people who express a new reality by which they have been grasped. Only this is what the church really means. It is the place where the power of the New Reality, which is Christ, and which was prepared in all history and especially in the Old Testament history, moves into man's situation and is continued by man. It is, again, the place where the New Being is real, and the place where one can go to make the New Being an actuality. It is in this sense the continuation of the New Being even if its organization seems always a betrayal of the New Being. That New Being which is behind all this is the divine being-itself, who is the foundation and Lord of both church and the spiritual community, visible as well as invisible.

B. Culture

One of the unique distinctions Tillich attained for himself as a philosophical theologian was his constant willingness to come out of

---

[29] *Theology of Culture*, pp. 41 and 212. Compare also with "A Reinterpretation of the Doctrine of the Incarnation," *Church Quarterly Review*, January-March, 1949, p. 149; "The Present Theological Situation in the Light of the Continental Development," *Theology Today*, October, 1949, p. 306; and "Reply to Interpretation and Criticism," *The Theology of Paul Tillich*, p. 338.

the theological circles to have a dialogue with other disciplines such as political science, medicine, particularly psychiatry and psychotherapy, art, and sociology. In fact it is crystal clear to all those who study his theology that one of his perennial concerns was to urge the theologians of all faiths to come out of their secluded theological "ivory towers" to have living dialogue with the so-called secular world. Although the church is not of the world, it is in the world, and indeed it is very much a part of this world with all its ambiguities, distorted marks, and secularism. It is against this totally autonomous world that Tillich sounded his warning tirelessly and urged people to see the signs of a coming new age—a theonomous age—for which they must be well prepared. In order to accomplish this enormous task, theology must recognize the interdependence among all the fields of the life process and construct the bridges through which the preparedness for a new kairos can be made attainable. In Tillich's mind, not only theological problems, but also sociological problems, psychological problems, problems of modern art, and problems of modern science are all involved in the question of the ultimate concern. The unconditional character of this religious concern in every branch of human pursuit implies that it refers to every moment of man's life, to every space and every realm. The whole universe is God's sanctuary, as the Psalmist exclaims. "Every work day is the day of the Lord, every supper a Lord's supper, every work the fulfillment of a divine task, every joy a joy in God. In all preliminary concerns, ultimate concern is present, consecrating them."[30]

Before proceeding any further, however, it is well to know how Tillich defined culture. Culture, he said, "is that which takes care of something, keeps it alive, and makes it grow."[31] In this way, man can cultivate everything he encounters, but in doing so, he does not leave the cultivated object unchanged; he creates something new from it—materially, as in language and the technical acts; receptively, as in cognitive and aesthetic acts; or reactively, as in personal and communal acts. In each of these three cases, culture creates something new beyond the encountered reality. It is, in sum, the self-creativity of life under the dimension of the spirit. On another occasion, Tillich defined it as "the totality of forms in which the basic concern of religion expresses itself"[32] and religion as ultimate concern is the meaning-giving-

---

[30] *Theology of Culture*, p. 41. See also "Speech at the Conference on the Ministry," Union Theological Seminary, March 27, 1953, p. 5.
[31] *ST III*, p. 57.
[32] *Theology of Culture*, p. 42.

substance of culture. In abbreviation: religion is the substance of culture, and culture is the form of religion.[33] This leads right into the discourse of relationship between religion and culture.

If it is maintained that culture is the level on which man creates himself whereas it is in religion that he receives the divine self-manifestation, which gives religion ultimate authority over culture, then destructive conflicts inevitably appear between religion and culture. Tillich tried hard to replace the noun, "level," with "dimension" as far as the relation between religion and culture and the mystery of life is concerned.[34] As the interpretation of his now renowned aphorism (renowned at least among the students and followers of his theological system): religion is the substance of culture, and culture is the form of religion, he suggested a consideration of religion as the principle which gives ultimate meaning to all cultural forms, or as the ultimate concern underlying every creative culture. There is no creative activity which can be performed apart from the creative ground of being, he insisted. This means that there is no cultural work completely excluded from religion, in the broader sense of the word.

Writing on "Religion in Relation to Morality and Culture," in *Systematic Theology III*,[35] Tillich insisted that in accordance with their essential nature, morality, culture, and religion interpenetrate each other. They constitute the unity of the spirit wherein the elements are distinguishable but not separable. The religious element in culture is the fathomless depth of a genuine creation. One may call it substance or the ground from which culture is nourished. It is the element of ultimacy which culture lacks itself but to which it points its finger. Religion, which is the self-transcendence of life under the dimension of the eternal, is related to culture in the depth of profundity. Thus, without its religious substance, culture is left with an increasingly empty form, but with it culture receives meaning, seriousness, and depth and creates out of its own material a religious culture of its own—a theonomous culture in which may be found the duality of religious and secular culture with innumerable transitions between them.

Tillich himself noted that "the problem of religion and culture has always been in the center of (my) interest,"[36] and that most of his

---

[33] *Ibid.*; and "Christian Criteria for Our Culture," *Criterion*, October, 1952, p. 1.

[34] See "Dimensions, Levels, and the Unity of Life," *Kenyon Alumni Bulletin*, October-December, 1959, pp. 4-8.

[35] *ST III*, pp. 94ff.

[36] *Theology of Culture*, Foreword v.

writings, including the two (by now three) volumes of *Systematic Theology*, try to define the way in which Christianity is related to secular culture. Contributing an article to *The Christian Century* in late 1960, he expressed explicitly his life-long devotion to the self-assigned job of bridging the gap between religion and culture in order that a theonomous culture can be created out of the secular and secularized culture. He concluded the article with the following sentences:

> 'Religion and Culture' is the title of a series of lectures I have given under the auspices of the humanities department of the (Harvard) college . . . it is my impression that the emphasis on the whole complex of problems indicated by the title 'Religion and Culture' is at the center of college work in religion all over the country. This is somehow a fulfillment of a main trend in my whole life work. . . . It is my desire to work in this direction with the remainder of time and strength which is given to me.[37]

Without any exception, a theonomous culture expresses in its creations an ultimate concern and a transcending meaning not as something strange (heteros) but as its own spiritual depth. The idea of a theonomous culture does not imply, therefore, any imposition from outside. It is the spirit-determined and spirit-directed culture, and the Spirit always fulfills spirit instead of breaking it. "The idea of theonomy is (thus) not antihumanistic, but it turns the humanistic indefiniteness about the 'where-to' into a direction which transcends every particular human aim."[38] It turns the self-wandering and other-determined cultures to the insight to be reoriented with that which is the highest, and at the same time the deepest, in a vertical line. Theonomy inserts (back) into all cultures their spiritual substance, the center of meaning, and their continuous reference to the ultimate. It bestows the spirituality to culture, although the term "spirituality of culture" could give the impression that culture should be dissolved into religion. The term "self-transcendence of culture" therefore could be more adequate. Its meaning at any rate is the state of culture under the impact of the Spiritual Presence, giving all preliminary meanings depth and all finite concerns ultimate seriousness.

Tillich advocated the idea that to give general characteristics of a theonomous culture apart from its particular functions is difficult, but

---

[37] "On the Boundary Line," *The Christian Century*, December 7, 1960, p. 1437.
[38] *ST III*, pp. 250f.

that one may point to certain qualities of theonomy which are derived from its very nature. They are:

> First of all, the style, the over-all form, of theonomous works of cultural creation expresses the ultimacy of meaning even in the most limited vehicles of meaning—a painted flower, a technical tool, a form of social intercourse. . . . None of these things is unconsecrated in a theonomous situation. . . . The second quality is the affirmation of the autonomous forms of the creative process. Theonomy would be destroyed the moment in which a valid logical conclusion was rejected in the name of the ultimate to which theonomy points, and the same is true in all other activities of cultural activity. . . . The third characteristic of theonomy (is) its permanent struggle against both an independent heteronomy and an independent autonomy.[39]

A period that is turned toward, and open to, the unconditional is one in which the consciousness of the presence of the unconditional permeates and guides all cultural forms and functions, and with this divine nature mixed with, and dwelling within, the temporal things. Theonomous as applied to culture has the meaning of the paradoxical phrase "transcendental culture."[40]

III. THEONOMY AND HISTORY

A. Theonomous Interpretation of History

Tillich taught that theonomy is inseparably related to human history. To Tillich, theonomy gives a key to the interpretation of history, because it can characterize a whole cult and all of the historical phenomena. "History comes from and moves toward periods of theonomy, i.e., periods in which the conditioned is wide open to the unconditional without any claim to be unconditioned itself." Thus theonomy "unites the absolute and the relative element in the interpretation of history."[41] This is so simply because eternity transcends and at the same time contains temporality, but in this theonomous 'eternal now' the 'now,' or temporality, is no longer subject to the law of finite transitoriness. It takes into itself a transcendental nature—the kairos element of, and in, time and history. In that moment the past and future are

---

[39] *Ibid.* Note: Readers are referred to Chapter III, I, A, The Meaning and Characteristics of Theonomy.
[40] *ST III*, p. 266.
[41] *The Protestant Era*, p. 47.

united, though not negated in the eternal presence. History then moves toward its end. "The eternal participates in the moments of time, judging and elevating them to the eternal."[42] The ultimate meaning of history can be seen only from this suprahistorical perspective. That is to say, through its three-fold functions in history—as fulfillment, unification, and purification. Theonomy, by throwing out all the ambiguities of life momentarily, is the answer to the riddle of history. It is the sacred "unification and purification of all elements of preliminary meaning which have become embodied in historical activities and institutions." Tillich continued, "in so far as this unity and purity lie beyond history we have to state that the meaning of history transcends history."[43] It is a dynamic power acting in history, materializing itself in history although never becoming identical with history. Tillich observed that history is not, and never can be, completed but is always becoming; that it always has an expectant attitude, and is always "at hand," ready for a theonomous invasion. This means that God—the only true God—is a living God, entering into and struggling in history and fulfilling it in the course of the process. To sum it up, it is Tillich's view that "theonomy . . . is the substance and meaning of history," and thus he urged man to "plunge more deeply into the ground of our historical life, into the ultimate depth of history."[44]

B. THEONOMY, THE NEW BEING, AND KAIROS

A theonomous interpretation of Tillich's view of history cannot be accomplished aside from his concepts of New Being and kairos. In fact, it is inconceivable to understand Tillich's concept of theonomy apart from his ideas on the New Being as appeared in Jesus of Nazareth and kairos. It is the purpose of this subsection, therefore, to introduce and discuss these two ideas in Tillich's thought.

1. The New Being and Christ

The discussion of the New Being and Christ is further divided into the following two parts: a) Jesus Christ as the bearer of the New Being, and b) The unique characteristics of Christ as the New Being.

---

[42] *Biblical Religion and the Search for Ultimate Reality*, p. 78.
[43] "The Theology of Missions," *Christianity and Crisis*, April 4, 1955, p. 35; and *The Kingdom of God in History*, pp. 114f.
[44] *The Protestant Era*, p. 45; and *The Shaking of the Foundations*, p. 58, respectively.

a) Jesus Christ as the Bearer of the New Being

In Tillichian expression, the above heading might as well be rewritten as "Jesus as the Christ is the bearer of the New Being," or "New Being in Jesus as the Christ," which he called the material norm of Systematic Theology.[45] At any rate, regardless of which expression one wishes to employ, it bears witness to the close affinity between the two concepts, which requires most intimate scrutiny on man's part.

Against the estranged human existence the reality of the New Being is "a reality in which the self-estrangement of our existence is overcome, a reality of reconciliation and reunion, of creativity, meaning, and hope."[46] The New Being is based on what Saint Paul calls the "new creation" and refers to its power to overcome the demonic cleavages of the "old reality" in soul, society, and universe. This power in the New Being is fully and explicitly manifest in Jesus the Christ—the bringer of the new eon and new reality, who can also be symbolically called the Messiah, the man-from-above, the Son of God, the Spirit, the logos-who-became-flesh.[47] It is the task of the Messiah, the logos-on-earth, to conquer the existential estrangement of the human situation, and to establish a new reality from which the demonic powers or structure of destruction are excluded.

The indispensability of the appearance of the New Being lies in the universal longing for such a being, Tillich believed. After pursuing the ways of self-salvation—legalistic, ascetic, mystical, sacramental, doctrinal, and emotional—and seeing all of them fail, men throughout the world become aware of the need for a New Being. In every religion and in every autonomous or heteronomous culture there has been, Tillich observed, an expectation of a totally new reality from another dimension which would salvage and replace man's perverted reality. The quest for the New Being is universal because the human predicament is universal, he contended, even though the character of the quest differs from religion to religion and from culture to culture. It is nonetheless universal. It is in response to this existential quest that Christ comes to the world as the bearer and manifestation of the New Being.[48]

---

[45] *ST I*, p. 50.
[46] *ST I*, p. 49.
[47] *Ibid.*
[48] See *ST II*, pp. 81-86; and Bernard Martin, *The Existentialist Theology of Paul Tillich*, 1963, p. 159.

b) The Unique Characteristics of Christ as the New Being

Out of all the ramifications of Tillich's rich and complex treatment of the characteristics of Christ as the bearer of the New Being, or his abundant amplification of the doctrine of Christology—which occupies the entire *Systematic Theology II*—and numerous references to the concept of the New Being, this researcher concentrated only on two of the characteristics which are unique as far as the New Being is concerned. They are, firstly, the historicity of Jesus Christ as the New Being, and secondly, his complete and uninterrupted unity with God.

The discussion on the historicity of Jesus Christ inevitably involves occasional reference to the once-for-allness, or unrepeatability, of his appearance as the New Being. Tillich was cognizant of the fact that what distinguishes Christ as the New Being is the validity of the belief in his historical appearance in the form of a person, a real and complete person, without ceasing to be the Son of God from above; and that this event occurs—or to be more precise, can occur—only once in history. It is the moment of Kairos, with a capital K, and not a kairos, with a small k.[49] But yet, Tillich suggested that it is not even the most significant and unique of all the kairoi that have ever happened in history.[50]

Tillich emphatically maintained that in Jesus God had indeed appeared to man in a human life. This human life is called Messiah, Christos, because it represents the divine beyond and against human creatures. He appeared in history and beyond history, appearing once in history and ruling all history. Writing in the *Church Quarterly Review*, London, England, in 1949, Tillich upheld the view that the coming of the New Being in the person of Jesus as the Christ is an event in time and space and that it occurred but once, and is unrepeatable, possible only in a special situation and in a special, incomparable, individual form. He was a subject of eye-witness reports and not of analysis or deduction. Tillich continued: "The divine being, who like God is spiritual, becomes flesh, but without ceasing to be the Logos." The doctrine of the incarnation is centered on the extraordinary event

---

[49] For detailed development of the doctrine of kairos, see the next subsection.

[50] Note: For those who are interested in Tillich's utterances on the historicity of Jesus as the Christ, referral is made to: 1. "The Significance of the Historical Jesus for the Christian Faith," *Monday Forum Talks*, Union Theological Seminary, February 28, 1938. 2. "A Reinterpretation of the Doctrine of the Incarnation," *Church Quarterly Review*, January-March, 1949. 3. *ST II*, Part III, II, A, pp. 97-118, and 125-135.

in which is found "the creation of a new reality within and under the conditions of man's predicament."[51]

Basing his judgment on the foregoing references in the above two paragraphs, this researcher strongly rejects the criticism and rebukes voiced by some established scholars[52] who stated that Tillich did not emphasize the historicity of Christ as the New Being. Tillich stated adequately enough his belief in the reality of the historical Jesus as the bearer of the divine reality who, as the New Being, restores the broken relationship between man and God. He declared that by Christ's living in man's midst he demonstrated the genuine agape which God holds for man. Without the historical factuality of Jesus Christ, God's scheme for man would stop short of becoming a reality, a true salvation, according to Tillich.

The other characteristic which belongs singularly to Jesus is his complete and uninterrupted unity with the ground of being. Both adjectives here used in connection with the unity must be distinctively emphasized and maintained. The unity between Jesus as the Christ and his heavenly Father was complete and absolute, whereas even at the strongest theonomous moment man's unity with God through the reconciliatory power of the New Being is incomplete, partial, and fragmentary. The picture of the New Being in Jesus as the Christ is that of a figure with serious temptations, struggles, and tragic involvement in the ambiguities of life, however.

> It is the picture of a personal life which is subjected to all the consequences of existential estrangement but wherein estrangement is conquered in himself and a permanent unity is kept with God. Into this unity he accepts the negativities of existence without removing them. This is done by transcending them in the power of this unity.[53]

The complete unity with God in Jesus was kept in spite of his finitude and the overwhelming power of demonic temptations and constant threats, because he was able to sacrifice himself continuously as Jesus to himself as the Christ.

This continuous effort in faith by Jesus is the reason for his unin-

---

[51] "A Reinterpretation of the Doctrine of the Incarnation," *Church Quarterly Review*, January-March, 1949, p. 135; and *Theology of Culture*, p. 40, respectively.

[52] Tavard, *op. cit.*, p. 167; Martin, *op. cit.*, p. 178; and Nels F. S. Ferré, "Three Critical Issues in Tillich's Philosophical Theology," *Scottish Journal of Theology*, September, 1957, p. 236.

[53] *ST II*, p. 135.

terrupted unity with God. His faith and trust in God were never-ceasing and ever-present, in sharp contrast to man's on both accounts. By maintaining the complete unity with God uninterruptedly, he was able to keep the theonomous state unbroken at any time. This was possible, not because he was truly God but only half human, as Docetics taught, but was due entirely to his never-changing faith in God from the bottom of his heart and the center of his being in its totality.[54] In its totality; yes, this is another mark of him who is called the Christ in whom the New Being has shone through. Jesus as the Christ is the bearer of the New Being in its totality—in all of Jesus' words, deeds, and suffering[55] —not in any special or partial expressions of him. The wholesome and complete unity Jesus maintained with being-itself is exemplary of the ultimate concern man should have with his ground of being. What differentiates man from Jesus is the fact that while Jesus was able to keep this unity throughout his life, man can succeed only temporarily, sporadically, and fragmentarily.

2. Kairos

a) The Meaning of the Term

In order to comprehend the meaning of the term, kairos, in Tillich's thinking, one must first of all be able to differentiate the meanings between the words kairos and chronos, both of which can be translated into English as "time." For this purpose, one may go to the *Handbook of Christian Theology*, edited by Marvin Halverson, in 1958, for which Tillich contributed an article entitled Kairos. In this article he defined chronos (χρονος) as designating "the continuous flux of time . . . (pointing) to the measurable side of the temporal process—clock time." It is the "quantitative, calculable, repetitive element of the temporal process."[56] Or again, it can be defined simply, "a formal time."

In contrast with these elements which Tillich attributed to the term chronos, he said that kairos "points to unique moments in the temporal process, moments in which something unique can happen or be accomplished." As such, kairos emphasizes the qualitative, experiential, unique element. It is, again, "the right time, the moment rich in content and significance . . . qualitative and full of significance," or, "the fate of

---

[54] *ST II*, p. 138. Compare also with *ST I*, p. 137.
[55] *Ibid.*, pp. 121-123.
[56] Marvin Halverson, ed., *Handbook of Christian Theology*, p. 194. Also *ST III*, p. 369.

the time, the point at which time is disturbed by eternity."[57] In Tillich's linguistic analysis, the English word timing catches better than any other word the meaning of kairos.[58] It is God's providential timing that makes fulfilled an event, age, or even a person, and relates it to the unconditioned.

Kairos, as time, has closest affinity with history, according to Tillich, because it is the moment selected to become the center of history. "The moment at which history, in terms of a concrete situation, had matured to the point of being able to receive the break-through of the eternal manifestation of the Kingdom of God,"[59] wrote Tillich, which is the "fulfillment of time" according to the New Testament and "kairos" in the Greek language. When one is grasped by the power of kairos, he is in contact with a suprahistorical reality, although the historicity of the event is not negated, and experiences the presence of the past in the present. In that ecstatic moment he is taken into the dynamic advent of the eternal in and through temporality. Yet there is required in this divine-human historical encounter a preparedness on man's part. Tillich alluded to the fact that kairos is the description of the moment in which the eternal breaks into history and demands a decisive step, and the temporal is well prepared to receive it.[60] When Jesus said "The time is fulfilled, and the Kingdom of God is at hand," he meant that God's timing is about to break into human timing; that something new that is of an eternal nature is to appear at any moment. Note, however, that Jesus did not conclude his preaching there. He continued, saying, "Repent ye, and believe the gospel."[61] That meant the necessity and indispensability of man's preparedness to receive the "good news." It is evident from the foregoing explanations that the kairos moment is full of tensions, potentialities, and even dangers. This point will be dealt with in the last of the subsections, under the heading, A-kairos.

b) Kairos, kairoi, and history

Straightforwardly Tillich identified the coming of Jesus as the moment of Kairos, with a capital K. The life of all Christendom is fo-

---

[57] Halverson, Ibid.; The Protestant Era, p. 33; and The Interpretation of History, p. 174, respectively.
[58] Ibid.; ST III, p. 369; and The New Being, p. 161.
[59] ST III, p. 369. Compare "The Present Theological Situation in the Light of the Continental European Development," Theology Today, October, 1949, p. 303.
[60] The Interpretation of History, p. 93. Also "Trends in Religious Thought that Affect Social Outlook," Religion and World Order, 1943, p. 28.
[61] The Gospel of Mark 1: 15.

cused on the unique event in which the appearance of Christ took place. For Christian faith, this event is the Kairos in its unique and universal sense, making it the center of history and determining the beginning, the end, and the meaning of history.[62] God was always in Jesus and he was completely possessed by the divine Spirit at every moment of his earthly life. In possessing him, the Spirit gave him the certainty about the right hour, the kairos, for acting and suffering. And by being the embodiment of the New Being for historical mankind at the appointed time, Jesus established the center of history once and for all.[63]

This great Kairos, or basic Kairos, presupposes many smaller kairoi within the historical development. In other words, in order for the great Kairos to be received, many smaller kairoi are required in the historical development following it. Otherwise the central Kairos loses its concreteness and applicability to the history of mankind. The unique appearance of the New Being in the great Kairos thus supplemented by smaller kairoi creates centers of lesser importance on which the periodization of history is dependent. Their relationship is the relationship of the criterion to that which stands under the criterion and the relationship of the source of power to that which is sustained by the source of power. Together they, the great Kairos and the kairoi, determine the course and dynamics of history in its self-transcendence. They are the moments in which the theonomous manifestation of the Kingdom of God is apparent and the purification and unification of history become possible. Tillich believed that the Kingdom of God is always present, but the experience or awareness of its history-shaking power is not, and it is due to their combined effect that one can be opened to the grips of the eternal power.[64]

To mention a few of the specific characteristics of kairoi, one must note first of all that they are the continually recurring and deviative moments in which a religious or cultural group has an existential encounter with the central event in history, namely, the appearance of Jesus Christ as the embodiment of the New Being. An encounter of this sort is the basis for creating a spiritual community. Second, the deviative nature of kairoi implies that every kairos is implicitly and potentially a universal kairos and an actualization of the unique Kairos, the establishment of the center of history. However, one must hasten to add that under the existential circumstances, there is, and can be, no kairos which

---

[62] Halverson, op. cit., p. 195; and The Protestant Era, p. 46.
[63] ST III, p. 144.
[64] The Protestant Era, Introduction, xv; also ST III, pp. 140 and 370.

brings the perfect fulfillment in time. Nevertheless, it is due to these kairoi that the universal and unique Kairos is retrospectively reproduced to bestow the substance to a given period. Third, these outstanding moments in the temporal process can be called kairoi purely because, like the central Kairos, they are the moments in which the eternal breaks into the temporal, shaking and transforming it and creating a crisis in the depth of human existence. The creation of the crisis calls for another kairos to come to its rescue and by reaching the very depth of an autonomous reason, a theonomous state is being created.[65]

As a keen analyst of culture and religion, Tillich had much to say about the relationship between kairos and the modern age. It was his observation that an epochal moment of history is visible today, and that a new theonomous age is at hand. The theonomously-oriented kairos moment will conquer the destructive gap between religion and secular culture and cleanse the secularized and emptied autonomous culture for the sake of refilling it with divine substance and direction. It is with this insight that Tillich founded the "Kairos Circle" which tried to warn the present generation against the dangers of identifying the finite with the infinite and also against man's extreme reliance upon his own autonomous creative powers as final and absolute in solving human problems of this age. Through the series of crises and catastrophes that the present generation has witnessed, Tillich saw an emerging kairos with its powers of both destruction and creation, criticism and reconstruction. He felt quite sure that a theonomous age lies in the not-too-distant future and urged his contemporaries to be prepared to serve the logos out of the depths of their souls.[66]

c) A-kairos

Before concluding this chapter, a few words must be said on the concept of a-kairos in Tillich's thinking. Tillich recognized, perhaps more than anyone else, that in the history of mankind there has been ample historical evidence to prove that a kairos was often misinterpreted, or that the moment of kairos was misjudged and a wrong moment therefore was taken as the manifestation of a kairos. Tillich called this kind of misinterpretation or misjudgment on man's part a-kairos. To quote him:

> Two things must be said about kairoi: first, they can be demonically distorted, and second, they can be erroneous. . . . The error

---

[65] See *ST III*, p. 153; and *The Protestant Era*, pp. 45 and 47.
[66] *The Protestant Era*, pp. 15 and 59; and *The Religious Situation*, p. 52.

lies not in the kairos-quality of the situation but rather in the judgment about its character in terms of physical time, space, and causality, and also in terms of human reaction and unknown elements in the historical constellation.[67]

Tillich cited the appearance and ascendance of Nazism under Hitler in the early 1930s as a good example on this score. The Germans of three decades ago mistook his escalation to power and his ability to conquer the neighbouring nations as a sign of the kairos in the twentieth century and that they were the chosen people to accomplish the unification and purification of the world. They a-kairosized the appearance of Der Führer as a kairos, directly for the German nation and indirectly for all nations. Evidently it was a-kairos because they, while claiming a kairos in their midst, attacked the great Kairos and everything for which it stands.[68]

A-kairos can happen not only in the secular world but also in the religious sphere, Tillich emphasized. Speaking to theological circles in 1963, he stated that a theology which does not deal seriously with the criticism of religion by secular thought and some particular forms of secular thought and some particular forms of secular faith, such as "liberal humanism, nationalism, and socialism, would be 'a-kairos'— missing the demand of the historical moment."[69]

Writing in *The Protestant Era*, Tillich wondered aloud: Is it possible that the message of the kairos is an error? The message is always in error, he replied to himself, for it will be fulfilled only in long periods of time. And yet the message of kairos is never an error—it is always present.[70]

---

[67] *ST III*, p. 371.

[68] *Ibid.* Also "The Present Theological Situation in the Light of the Continental European Development," *Theology Today*, October, 1949, p. 303.

[69] *Ibid.*, p. 6.

[70] *The Protestant Era*, p. 51.

CHAPTER IV

Autonomy and Heteronomy

For the sake of expedience, this chapter is divided into the following two major sections: I. Autonomy. II. Heteronomy.

I. AUTONOMY

What is hoped to be accomplished in this section is, firstly, to discover the meaning and determine the nature of autonomy as expounded in Tillich's written work and, secondly, to relate this idea to the main concept in this thesis—the concept of theonomy in Paul Tillich.

A. THE MEANING AND NATURE OF AUTONOMY

The etymology of the word, autonomy, reveals that it is composed of two Greek words, αυτος (self), and νομος (law). The meanings of nomos have been explained in the preceding chapter under the title, Tillich's Concept of Theonomy; consequently, what is necessary here is the semantic clarification of the word autos. Autos, according to Souter's lexicon previously cited, has a threefold meaning: (a) he; (b) self; with a definite article, ὁ (the), following it, it means 'the very', but is often weakened to mean simply 'that,' meaning 'that self'; (c) with ὁ preceding it, autos means 'the same.'[1] The English word, automation, which attained its significance in industry, labor, and business, and its popularity in the everyday life of America only a few decades ago, is derived from the Greek word, αυτοματος = αυτος, which should linguistically be translated as 'of his own accord.'[2]

---

[1] Souter, op. cit., p. 43.

[2] Note: In The Gospel of St. John 16: 27, it is written: "For the Father himself loveth you . . ." which according to the Greek New Testament is, "αυτος γαρ ὁ πατηρ φιλει υμας . . . ." The English word 'himself' here should have been translated 'of his own accord,' according to the definitions in Souter's lexicon.

Tillich taught that autonomy does not mean the absolute freedom of the individual to be a law to himself. It means rather the obedience of the individual to the law of reason, which he finds in himself as a rational being. "The nomos ('law') of autos ('self') is not the law of one's personality structure. It is the law of subjective-objective reason; it is the law implied in the logos structure of mind and reality"[3] and thus autonomy resists with adequate power the danger of being engulfed by the predicament of man in existence. Tillich had much to say about the logos, the universal reason, in connection with an autonomous man. Speaking to a Japanese audience on the basic ideas of Religious Socialism in the Spring of 1960, he spoke of autonomy to mean that man has within himself the law of universal reason and follows its own structure without accepting any interference, be it from his own desires or fears, or be it from any outside authority.[4] More detailed discourse will be made on the relationship between autonomy and heteronomy (strange or outside law) in II, C, of the present chapter but let it be said at this juncture that, to Tillich, autonomy simply means "obedience to reason,"[5] that is, to make oneself obeisant to the logos, the universal reason, which is immanent in reality and mind and that man must, out of ontological spontaneity, obey and follow its forms, structures, and laws with volitional willingness. It is the obedient acceptance of the forms, structures, and laws of logos with their unconditional characters as the principles that control the realms of individual and social culture, and, as such, as the norms of truth and justice, of order and beauty, of personality and community.[6]

Autonomy operates in theoretical as well as practical spheres of culture, both individual and social. To quote Tillich's own words again:

> It replaces mystical nature with rational nature . . . and in the place of the magical sense of communion it sets up technical control. It constitutes communities on the basis of purpose, and morality on the basis of individual perfection. It analyzes everything in order to put it together rationally. It makes religion a matter of personal decision and makes the inner life of the individual dependent upon itself. It releases also the forces of an autonomous political and economic activity.[7]

---

[3] ST I, p. 84. See also The Protestant Era, pp. 44f and 56; McKelway, op. cit., p. 79; and Kegley and Bretall, ed., op. cit., pp. 82 and 314.

[4] "The Basic Ideas of Religious Socialism," The Bulletin, The International House of Japan, Inc., October, 1960, p. 14. Refer also to the "Christian Criteria for Our Culture," Criterion, October, 1952, p. 3.

[5] The Protestant Era, pp. 44f.

[6] The Protestant Era, p. 45.

[7] Ibid., p. 44.

Man as a bearer of universal reason is evidently the source and measure of culture and religion. Theodor Siegfried, of the Department of Theology, the University of Marburg, Germany, writing on "Tillich's Theology for the German Situation," in *The Theology of Paul Tillich*, states that Tillich, in agreement with Saint Paul's letter to the Romans and with Kant, defined autonomy as the ability of man to discover the universal law of theoretical and practical reason in himself without dependance on heteronomous authorities of any sort.[8] This observation is confirmed by Tillich himself in at least two of his rather elaborate discussions on this score.[9]

B. AUTONOMY AND THEONOMY

Although a relationship between theonomy and heteronomy is not non-existent, as will be witnessed in this researcher's discoveries in section II of the present chapter, definitely safe is a statement that, for Tillich, there exist a closer relationship between theonomy and autonomy. This is attested by the abundance of references in Tillich's writings on the subject.[10]

Tillich frequently stressed most emphatically that theonomy is not a suppression of autonomy. In fact autonomy is always present as a tendency in a theonomous situation; it acts under the surface of every theonomy.[11] For further elucidation of this point, one can turn to the earliest of all the primary sources employed in this research, *The Religious Situation*, in which one reads the following sentences: There is a movement to and fro between self-transcendence and self-sufficiency, between the desire to be a mere vessel and the desire to be the content, between the turning toward the eternal and the turning toward the self. In this action and reaction we discern the religious situation of every present at its profoundest level.[12] As a matter of fact the most intimate motions within the depth of human souls are not completely man's own; they belong to the ground of all being which is the basis and destination as well of one's individual life. Being so often overly talkative and in motion on one's own superficial level, man very seldom

---

[8] Kegley and Bretall, ed., *op. cit.*, p. 82.
[9] See "The Special Character of Contemporary Culture," in *The Theology of Culture*, pp. 43-45; and "Man and History," in *ST III*, Part V, I, 1, pp. 300-313.
[10] To mention only a few: *The Religious Situation*, pp. 18, 39, and 153; *The Protestant Era*, pp. 44f, 56f, and 220f; *ST I*, pp. 83f, 147f, and 208; *ST III*, pp. 249ff; and *The Future of Religions*, pp. 86ff, etc.
[11] *The Religious Situation*, p. 39. See also *ST III*, p. 250.
[12] *Ibid.*, p. 46.

listens to the voices speaking to his depth and from his depth. Tillich argued insistently that the name of this infinite and inexhaustible depth and ground of all being is God. That depth is what the word God means.[13]

The power which oscillates between theonomy and autonomy exists because it is bestowed upon man by none other than the divine himself. Attributing it to God's utterance, Tillich wrote: I give the power to shake the foundations of your earth into your hands. Indeed throughout the centuries, man is perennially in quest of the divine, the transcendental but "this quest is possible only because the transcendental has already dragged us out beyond ourselves as we have received answers which drive us to the quest."[14]

A distorted autonomous person that can be found abundantly under the conditions of existence constantly repels that which comes from his own depth and tries desperately to be absolutely and completely on his own. To this kind of person, the "New Being in Christ" who comes from the being-itself is an offense against his unshaken reliance upon himself; it poses a threat with devastating power in his self-saving attempts. Over and against this kind of autonomous person, Tillich urged that man's faith in himself ought to be a faith and courage to affirm his own finitude; to transcend beyond his autonomous self; and to plunge deeply into the depth of his own soul that is the dwelling place of God. Tillich wrote:

> Faith comprises both itself and the doubt of itself. The Christ is Jesus and the negation of Jesus. . . . To live serenely and courageously in these tensions and to discover finally their ultimate unity in the depths of our own souls and in the depth of the divine life is the task and the destiny of human thought.[15]

One can become truly confident about his own existence only after ceasing to base his confidence in himself. It must be based on God and solely on God alone who is experienced in unique and personal encounter at the very depth of a soul.

C. On Reason—Autonomous and Theonomous

What this researcher attempts to do in this subsection is to discover Tillich's teaching on autonomous and theonomous reason. It is by no

---

[13] The Shaking of the Foundations, pp. 46, 55, and 57.
[14] Ibid., p. 4; and "What's Wrong with the Dialectical Theology?," Journal of Religion, April, 1935, p. 140, respectively.
[15] Biblical Religion and the Search for Ultimate Reality, p. 85.

means to enter into full discourse on Tillich's doctrine of reason, human or divine. Whoever is interested in the topic is referred to Part I, Reason and Revelation, in *Systematic Theology I.*

As was explained in Chapter III, theonomy cannot possibly come about without the receptive vessel as found in the faith of man. Tillich maintained that autonomous human reason is the precondition of faith in the divine and genuine faith is the human act in which reason transcends itself in ecstasy under the impact of the Spiritual Presence. Said he, "(For) only a being who has the structure of reason is able to be ultimately concerned . . . to be aware of the presence of the holy." Reason is the precondition of faith; faith the act in which reason reaches ecstatically beyond itself. "Reason can be fulfilled only if it is driven beyond the limits of its finitude, and experiences the presence of the ultimate, the holy."[16] Only the presence of the divine ground as it is manifested in Jesus as the Christ at the moment of kairos can award the spiritual substance to all forms and creations of human rationality; conversely, only theonomously inspired autonomous reason can explain and proclaim in depth the Christian message in its fullest sense. A theonomous, which is also termed by Tillich a self-transcending or ecstatic, reason alone possesses the capacity to receive the contents of faith.

Another definition Tillich bestowed on the term theonomy is that it is "autonomous reason united with its own depth." And what does the metaphor depth mean? It means that "the religious aspect points to that which is ultimate, infinite, unconditional in man's spiritual life."[17] At a theonomous moment reason actualizes, and thereby fulfills itself, in obedience to its own basic structural laws and in the power of its own inexhaustible ground; creating, as its natural result, a theonomous reason. Theonomy asserts that the laws and power are the innermost elements of man himself, rooted in the divine ground which is man's own ground. "The law of life transcends man," he said, "although it is, at the same time, his own."[18]

It is on the basis of this theological hypothesis that Tillich tried ceaselessly throughout all his life to prove, through his method of correlation, the interdependence and basic unity between theology—using theonomous reason[19]—and pure philosophy—employing autonomous

---

[16] *Dynamics of Faith*, pp. 76f.
[17] *Theology of Culture*, p. 7. Refer also to *ST I*, pp. 85 and 148.
[18] *The Protestant Era*, p. 57.
[19] *ST I*, p. 155.

reason[20]—in a theonomous situation. He stated that in a perfect theonomy the philosophical analysis of the structure of being-in-itself would be united with a theological expression of the meaning of being for man. The mutual immanence of theology and philosophy, though never perfect in human existence, is, in Tillich's terminology, a state of theonomy.[21] Philosophical search is generally and rightly conceived of as a search after truth in dependence on human reason, and reason alone. It is in this sense an anthropocentric enterprise, or in other words, humanistic self-elevation in knowledge and understanding. Yet in a theonomous situation

> cognitive reason does not . . . pursue knowledge for the sake of knowledge; it seeks in everything true an expression of the truth which is of ultimate concern, the truth of being as being, the truth which is present in the final revelation. Legal reason does not establish a system of sacred and untouchable laws . . . it relates the special as well as the basic laws of a society to the 'justice of the Kingdom of God' and to the Logos of being as manifest in the final revelation. Communal reason does not accept communal forms dictated by sacred ecclesiastical or political authorities . . . it relates them to the ultimate and universal community, the community of love, transforming the will to power by creativity and the libido by agape.[22]

It is the turning of man's endeavor toward the vertical line while preserving its humanness. In very general terms, the above quotation is the meaning of theonomy in Tillich.

D. FREEDOM, CONSCIENCE, AND THEONOMY

The unity between theonomy and the depth of autonomous reason cannot be brought to the fore without complete freedom on man's part. Even partial negation or suppression of human freedom brings forth only heteronomy, not theonomy. Furthermore, any prevention of the act of self-determination would destroy theonomy.[23] Concurring with the late Jewish philosopher, Martin Buber, Tillich stressed that the relationship between God and man is always an I-Thou relationship and at any given moment in which human freedom is limited, or the full exercise thereof is obstructed, a heteronomous situation is unavoidably

---

[20] *Ibid.*, pp. 18-28; and *The Protestant Era*, pp. 83-93.
[21] Kegley and Bretall, ed., *op. cit.*, p. 336.
[22] *ST I*, p. 149. Compare with *ST III*, p. 250.
[23] *ST III*, p. 251.

created which prohibits the rich realization of a theonomous kairos moment. In fact the creation of theonomy presupposes man's freedom even to reject theonomy itself, or at least to resist it. Theonomy can be brought to the surface with its efficacy only after the power of human resistance is exhausted and the "good news" from the ultimate dimension breaks through.[24] In that instant man becomes a centered existence without the slightest trace of internal chaos or distortion of any sort.

A man with total freedom means also a man with a clear and autonomous conscience. One of the indispensable prerequisites for a man to become theonomous—or, to put it more aptly, to have theonomous moments hold firm grips on his life—is to possess such a state of mind as to let the eternal speak freely to and to shine through it. In one of his best friends, Dr. Karen Horney, Tillich found such a mind. In his address at her funeral services, Tillich preached: She heard the sound of the eternal in (these) last years. But the power of the eternal was always working in her. For the manifestation of the eternal light and love worked in her and through her in all periods of her life.[25] In the October issue of the *Crozer Quarterly*, published by the Crozer Theological Seminary in Chester, Pennsylvania, in 1945, Tillich contributed an article on "The Conscience in Western Thought and the idea of a Transmoral Conscience" in which the author made a brief historical survey on the topic in question in the beginning. He then proposed that there must be a conscience which transcends the spheres of morality, law, or the commandments. He designated such a conscience, with its sparks from divine, a transmoral conscience. Said he: A conscience may be called transmoral which does not judge in obedience to a moral law but according to the participation in a reality which transcends the sphere of moral commands. Such a conscience breaks through the boundaries of law and rigidity and creates a joyful conscience.[26] The creation of such a free, spontaneous, and happy conscience is not restricted to individuals alone; in fact theonomy is a moment or an age when a social conscience is awakened and created in all groups under the spiritual impact be it movements, communities, or configuration of independent individuals.[27]

E. Autonomous Culture and Theonomy

A few words must be said on the relationships and interrelationships of an autonomous culture and theonomy before this section on auton-

---

[24] See *ST II*, p. 8 and *ST III*, p. 370.
[25] *Pastoral Psychology*, May, 1953, p. 12.
[26] *Crozer Quarterly*, October, 1945, pp. 297 and 300.
[27] *ST III*, p. 247.

omy is concluded. A brief description of the relationship between culture and theonomy was made in Chapter III, Section II, B, pp. 23-27 of the present thesis; nevertheless, let it be noted at this point that one of Tillich's major interests as a philosophical theologian was the analysis of autonomous culture as vividly detectable in the Western hemisphere and, by so doing, to urge incessantly a self-evaluation and self-criticism of the modern purely anthropocentric culture for the purpose of elevating it to a theonomous height. Notwithstanding the fact that the coming of theonomy depends wholly on God's grace alone, i.e., in his appointed time, as was discussed in Chapter III, Section III, B, pp. 28-36, there is required at the same time a response, or reaction, on man's part, as was explained in the same chapter, Section I, C, pp. 20-21. What Tillich tirelessly strived to accomplish in the past half century was to arouse people's awareness of the role man must play in a theonomous dialogue and, even more, to go further in preparing for the kairos moment with absolute concern.

The motive of this endeavor was based on his observation that the basic unity between theonomy and autonomy is so often disrupted, the cause of which is attributable to the ambiguities of human existence in its distorted form and the eruption of which is detectable easily in the vital yet aimless forms of contemporary cultural manifestations. Tillich did not hesitate in pinpointing autonomy as the direct cause of this disappearance of the theonomous stage in history. In *The Protestant Era*, he inquired: How could such a stage in history disappear? What has destroyed theonomy? The answer is the always present, always driving, always restless principle of autonomy. Moreover, the nature of this disunity is such that whenever and wherever the "(theonomous) power is broken, it cannot be re-established as it was, the road must be traveled to its very end, namely, to the moment in which a new theonomy appears in a new kairos."[28] Throughout the history of civilization, both in East and West, Tillich fumed, the self-complacent autonomous creations repeatedly severed the ties of a civilization with its ultimate ground and meaning, whereby, to the extent in which it succeeded, a civilization became exhausted, spiritually empty, and withered away. The history of autonomous cultures is a history of continuous waste of spiritual substance and at the end of this process the culture turns its eyes back to the lost theonomous period with impotent longing, or it looks eagerly

---

[28] *The Protestant Era*, p. 46.

forward to a new theonomy in an attitude of creative waiting until a kairos reappears.[29]

As a prophet in his own right, Tillich regarded the contemporary period as a period in which the following elements, particularly in the Western world, are embraced: (1) The modern age is in a state of total spiritual exhaustion, and (2) It is looking for a new theonomy to invade into it and elevate it to a new height and depth. The Western culture is not alone in this aspect. Tillich observed after careful analysis that the ancient civilizations represented by Greek and Roman empires trod the same path the modern capitalist and technological society is treading. In sharp contrast with the periods when the theonomous element was so strong that autonomy could not even start, as in many primitive cultures, these completely autonomous cultures became victorious in their conflict with theonomous elements in the course of history and pushed the latter into the underground of cultural expressions of a particular period.[30] The capitalist society is an extreme example of such a culture with its almost insurmountably fortified faith in the self-sufficiency of a human and finite world and also with its hope and purpose solely on the establishment of human control over the world of nature and mind. It is the best example of a self-assertive, self-sufficient type of existence. Tillich elaborated on this kind of autonomous culture with the sentences quoted below:

> This applies to mathematical natural science which pursues the goal of demonstrating that reality is governed wholly by its own laws and is rationally intelligible . . . It applies to world-ruling technique with its will to conquer space, time and nature and to make the earth a well-furnished dwelling of man. It applies, finally, to capitalist economy . . . to arouse and to satisfy ever increasing demands without raising the question as to the meaning of the process which claims the service of all the spiritual and physical human abilities.[31]

It is an attitude of life which makes man the measure of his own spiritual life—in art and philosophy, in science and politics, in social relations and personal ethics. Such an autonomous philosophy of life assumes that the divine is fully manifest in the human; that the ultimate concern of man is man.[32]

---

[29] Ibid.
[30] The Protestant Era, p. 45; and ST III, p. 250.
[31] The Religious Situation, p. 47.
[32] Dynamics of Faith, p. 63.

II. HETERONOMY

This section on heteronomy is discussed under the following three
subsections. A. The meaning and nature of the term, heteronomy. B.
Heteronomous authority, law, and church. C. Heteronomy, autonomy,
and theonomy.

A. The Meaning and Nature of the Term, Heteronomy

Semantically analyzed, the term, heteronomy, is derived from two
Greek words, ἕτερος (else) and nomos. Tillich simply stated that heteronomy is man's subjection to authority, or a strange law. He then elaborated it by defining heteronomy as "the authority claimed or exercised
by a finite being in the name of the infinite."[33]

According to the Greek lexicon previously referred to,[34] heteros
should appropriately be translated as (a) another, a second, or of the
two, (b) other or different. Returning to Tillich's usage of it, the term
heteros signifies the situation in which a law from outside, or a strange
law, is imposed on man and destroys, as its natural consequence, autonomy, or the inner law, of cultural and religious creativity. In so
doing, it demolishes the honesty of truth and the dignity of moral personality. It undermines creative freedom and the humanity of man. Its
symbol is the "terror" exercised by absolute authorities, religious or
secular. Heteronomy is the form in which "many rather conditioned
ideas and methods have been imposed on individuals and groups in
the name of an unconditioned truth, authoritatively and through suppression."[35] Camouflaging in the 'costume' of authority, Tillich mur-
mured, heteronomy exerts its power through the channels such as myths,
traditions, conventions, political and religious establishments, or cultic
mythologizing and practices. Or, it sometimes discharges its suppressive
functions through the systems of ethical rules or moral commands. It
is in accord with Tillich's interpretation that an 'alien law' can exercise its influence through just about any kind of worldly form: religious
authorities such as the Roman Catholic Church, quasi-religious authorities like the totalitarian governments, secular authorities as are manifested
in possessors of positive values such as family or school officialdom.

In his *Christianity and the Encounter of the World Religions*, pub-

---

[33] *ST I*, p. 148. Compare with "The Basic Ideas of Religious Socialism," *The
Bulletin*, The International House of Japan, Inc., October, 1960, p. 14.

[34] Souter, *op. cit.*, p. 98.

[35] *Theology of Culture*, pp. 135f.

lished in 1963, Tillich cited the best examples of such heteronomous authorities in Nazism and the totalitarian structure of Russian government. Linking the suppression of autonomous elements in these two ideological embodiments with an offer of an absolute, perfect future, he wrote on pages 6 and 7 the following words:

> This has been done, e.g., in Germany by the use of the old eschatological symbol of a "thousand-year period" for the future of Hitler's Reich, a symbol which originally signifies the aim of all human history. The same thing has been done in Russia in terms of Marxian type of eschatological thinking (classless society). In both cases it was necessary to deny the ambiguities of life and the distortions of existence within these systems . . . by glorifying the suppression of individual criticism and by justifying and systematizing lie and wholesale murder.

In Tillich's opinion, every finite and preliminary concern possesses a tyrannical element in demanding man's ultimate devotion and infinite concern. It keeps, or at least tries to keep, man in its bondage whenever he desires to free himself from it. Likewise, every finite thing—be it work, pleasure, money, science, another human being, or nation—in its twisted heteronomous form demands man's whole heart and his whole mind and his whole strength and orders him to transform it into his ultimate concern, i.e., his god. The power of a demonic heteronomy, moreover, is the power to turn the holy into a profane, the divine into an antidivine, and to falsify a preliminary concern to make it look like an ultimate concern. It will drive man to the point at which he loses the wisdom and rationality to distinguish between two fundamentally different entities and 'rhythms,' i.e., good and bad, divine and demonic, holy and profane, in life and in the course of history. By creating such a state of mind in man, it succeeds in inserting its alien law into his mind.[36]

One might be inadvertently misled to an impression from the above discourse that heteronomy superimposes its law, or laws, only from above, that is, from outside of the imposed. Tillich would have strongly repudiated this kind of interpretation should there be one. In fact, he would go as far as to claim that occasionally the heteronomous suppression is stronger when it comes from inner rather than from outer. In his comparatively recent volume, *Dynamics of Faith*, published in 1957, he argued with regard to the suppression of doubts and deviations by

---

[36] *The New Being*, pp. 157f.

fanaticism that they "were suppressed not only by external power but even more by the mechanisms of inner suppression. These mechanisms had been planted into the individual mind and were most effective even without pressure from outside."[37] This in essence is what he endeavored to convey when he spoke of a transmoral conscience within an individual, or theonomous ethics that transcends the realm of regulated good or righteous deeds.[38] As long as moralisms and ethics are confined within the limits of the imperative, they have an extremely volcanic tendency to become heteronomous because the more one disciplines himself to obey their commands, the stronger a force he will unintentionally cultivate within himself that it will emerge eventually as an irresistible force from within. It is quite natural that these moral or religious laws are usually set forth and imposed on the individuals by organized religious groups. The attention in the next step will focus on the relationships between heteronomous essence and authority, law, and church.

B. HETERONOMOUS AUTHORITY, LAW, AND CHURCH

In light of the discourses hitherto presented, it has been made clear that the relationship existing between culture, in its broadest sense, and religion is not exactly to be expressed in terms of affinity but should be in terms of interpenetration or interdependence. Where there is an ultimate concern there is religion—regardless of the socio-religious or mystic-aesthetic form in which it takes place. Tillich would unquestionably have gone so far as to declare that all the cultural and human creations are in fact religious creations in its broadest sense of the word. All the glories of human civilizations are, in this sense, religious glories. But, Tillich pointed out, beside religion's glories lie its shame. Because in its self-elevation and self-complacency, it glorifies its glory while forgetting the source of its glories. By tolerating this hubris[39] within it, religion makes itself the ultimate and despises the secular realm. It makes its myths and doctrines, rites and laws into ultimates and persecutes, or at least rejects, those who do not subject themselves to it.[40]

---

[37] *Dynamics of Faith*, p. 25.

[38] "Conscience in Western Thought and the Idea of a Transmoral Conscience," *Crozer Quarterly*, October, 1945, pp. 289-300; "Moralisms and Morality: Theonomous Ethics," *Theology of Culture*, pp. 133-145; and *Morality and Beyond*, 1963.

[39] Note: From Greek word, υβρις, which means the self-elevation of man to the sphere of the divine.

[40] *Theology of Culture*, p. 9.

In Christian terminology, it is the ecclesiastical heteronomy because it is in the form of an organized ecclesiastical (i.e., "a called out") church that these symbols, doctrines, rites, statutes, and laws are forced upon believers as well as non-believers. Among numerous forms of heteronomy—economic, political, educational, psychological, ideological, cultural, and religious[41]—religious heteronomy is most conspicuous and cruel in a great number of instances. Somehow, the Christian religion, in the form of its church, is willing to coerce people under the Christian 'yoke' in the name of the Perfect and Absolute and so, Tillich observed, one sees in all Christian churches the toiling and laboring of people who are called Christians, serious Christians, under innumerable laws which they cannot fulfill, from which they flee, to which they return, or which they replace by other laws. This is true not only on a theoretical basis but also on a practical level. These practical laws demand constant activities, active participation in religious and philanthropic enterprises, study of religious traditions, continuous prayers, meditations, and observation of the sacraments along with regular attendance in worship services. They also demand moral obedience, superhuman self-control and asceticism, devotion to man and things beyond one's possibilities, surrender to ideas and duties beyond one's power. They try to extract from people the power of unlimited self-negation, and unlimited self-perfection: the religious law demands the perfect in all respects. Under this heavy yoke of religion, Christians feel split, exhausted, and resentful. They try to throw them away, or to neglect them, or to be indifferent toward them. But they keep on coming back—to criticize, to interrogate, and to torment.[42]

So often these Christians are the people, because of their slavish condition under religious heteronomy, who will attempt to suppress their doubts or questions about their beliefs. The tool of repression is usually an acknowledged authority with certain sacred qualities such as the church, pope, or the Holy Scripture, to which one renders unconditional surrender. Or, not infrequently, they will resort to their tradition which is traced back, say, to the apostles, the church fathers, popes, reformers, or the founder of their own denomination. From this standpoint, which they maximize to the degree of absolute, they believe they possess all the truths and nothing but the truths without any need to worry about the question of absolute truth. Their truths, no matter whether they are based on a book developed and embraced by

---

[41] Read *The Protestant Era*, pp. 125ff.
[42] *The Shaking of the Foundations*, p. 98.

the members of their organization or are bestowed on a person, become the source of their worship and the symbols of servitude. Thus these finite objects are promoted to the infinite sphere and prevent an honest search after the immutable. To express it from a different vantage point of view, they become the weapons to split the souls of people between loyalty to the church and sincerity to truth. In this sense, Tillich reasoned, Jesus himself could have become an idol, following the fate of Jesus' own mother, Mary, with a majority of the Catholic believers. Or, Jesus could have become a national and racial hero to his own Jewish people.[43]

According to the Tillichian philosophy of history, there are periods in which theonomy is predominant, and in other periods, autonomy or heteronomy. It was his interpretation that the low Middle Ages were a heteronomous period in which theonomy was buried underground and autonomy was completely submerged. It was the time when demonization of the Roman Catholic Church had reached its climax which prompted the protest both of Reformation and Renaissance. It was also the period when masses were degraded to "subjects" only to work and obey without any power or right to resist the arbitrariness of their absolute rulers in princes and the ecclesiastical hierarchy. Catholicism then, and to a lesser degree even now, claimed to offer a secure way of overcoming the separation of man from his Creator through sacramental graces and ascetic exercises the efficacy of which was guaranteed by the hierarchy and its magical powers.[44]

Before leaving this subsection, attention must be given to the Protestant principle which arose against a heteronomous church at the end of the Middle Ages. Repeatedly,[45] Tillich pronounced that it is the Protestant principle that destroys holy superstitions, sacramental magic, and sacred heteronomy and that it is a divinely inspired and oriented prophetic protest against any hierarchical system which sets itself between God and man with a demonic claim to absoluteness. It was at the Reformation in the early sixteenth century that the prophetic spirit in the form of the Protestant principle attacked a demonically perverted priestly system, refusing to render to Satan what rightly belonged to God. The Protestant principle made crystal clear the distinction be-

---

[43] "Come and See," Sermon preached at Union Theological Seminary, New York, March 27, 1949.

[44] *The Courage to Be*, p. 61. Also *The Protestant Era*, p. 169.

[45] *ST III*, p. 134; *Dynamics of Faith*, p. 29; "The End of the Protestant Era," *The Student World*, The First Quarter, 1937, pp. 3-5, etc.

tween the finitude of the finite and the infinity of the eternal without confusing nor mixing them together. It was, and still is, the Protestant principle in and outside of the established church that points out the functions of all the things here on earth as something that have rootage in the ultimate and that they must not, therefore, claim any ultimacy.[46] It is a critical element in the expression of the community of faith and consequently the element of faith in the act of faith. As long as Christians possess and retain this principle, Tillich exhorted, they should not be worried about the state of the churches, about membership and doctrines, about the institutions and ministers, about sermons and sacraments. These can prove to be worthy things but these can also become 'circumcisions' that are superimposed upon men by a heteronomous church and the 'yoke' that Jesus Christ undertakes to get rid of from and for them.

C. Heteronomy, Autonomy, and Theonomy

It is in this subsection that comparison is being made of the assertive powers possessed by both heteronomy and autonomy and there are indicated points at which they differ from one another and conflict with each other. They are then related to the concept of theonomy. For the sake of clarity, the first portion of this subsection is set apart for discussion of the movement of heteronomy toward autonomy with a discussion of the 'attacks' from autonomy upon heteronomy to occupy the next portion and finally a few concluding words in relation to their mutual meeting ground, theonomy.

Tillich bluntly stated that heteronomous authorities are "the repression of and aggression toward autonomous thought," and in heteronomy "the broken symbols of myth and cult press in from the outside and prevent the mind from developing its autonomous structure."[47] Not singularly to repress an autonomous structure, heteronomy puts asunder

---

[46] Note: Although Tillich's system is very outspoken in its emphasis on the Protestant principle in Protestantism and Protestant churches, it has not ignored the demand that the "Catholic substance" be united with it. In his endeavor to unite the two, Tillich opened the way for the Roman Catholic Church to embrace the Protestant principle within it. See ST III, pp. 6 and 245. On the latter page, Tillich wrote that the Protestant principle is "effective in every church as the power which prevents profanization and demonization from destroying the Christian churches completely. It alone is not enough; it needs the 'Catholic substance,' the concrete embodiment of the Spiritual Presence . . ." See also Kegley and Bretall, ed., op. cit., p. 52.

[47] Dynamics of Faith, p. 53; and "Christian Criteria for Our Culture," Criterion, October, 1952, p. 3, respectively.

an autonomous, self-assured conscience also. For instance, in a collectivist society such as one sees in Soviet Russia or Red China, the lives of individuals are determined and manipulated by the existence and institutions of a group to the extent that all individual consciences must be suppressed and replaced by the group—i.e., the rulers'—conscience.[48] If one is to turn his eyes to the religious sphere he shall see that Tillich once vividly described religious heteronomy in the form of a written code, such as the Ten Commandments, the Mosaic laws as found in the Pentateuch, or The Sermon on the Mount in the New Testament. The devastatingly destructive power of a heteronomous religion can be visualized from the paragraph quoted below:

> The deadening power of the written code, written . . . into the unconscious depth of our being, recognized by our conscience, judging us by what we do, above all, by what we are. . . . And certainly, the written code in its threatening majesty . . . kills the joy of fulfilling our being by imposing upon us something we feel as hostile. It kills the freedom of answering creatively what we encounter in things and men by making us look at the table of laws . . . It kills our courage to act through the scruples of our anxiety-driven conscience. And among those who take it most seriously, it kills faith and hope, and throws them into self-condemnation and despair.[49]

Acknowledging the fact of countless millions who submit their autonomous sovereignty to a heteronomous imposition—even among the intellectuals[50]—Tillich nevertheless upheld the position that as divine creatures, man has the courage and power to follow one's own reason in defiance of an irrational authority. The prevalence of existentialism and secularism in recent decades proves this point most convincingly. It is the destiny of individual conscience that it cannot be satisfied with a suppressed state; sooner or later, it rebels against that which suppresses. Readers are referred to this researcher's discussion on the Protestant principle,[51] where it was described as a prophetic spirit that protests against any suppressor of an autonomous reason and conscience. This autonomous reason raises its voice irrepressibly to break the countless shackles that exist in a heteronomous society. It eliminates hundreds

48 The Courage to Be, p. 92.
49 The Eternal Now, pp. 89f.
50 "Religion and Intellectuals," Partisan Review, March, 1950, p. 256. Compare with The Courage to Be, p. 49, where he wrote: "In order to avoid the risk of asking and doubting he surrenders the right to ask and doubt."
51 Pages 100-102.

of means of oppression that exist in a church. It is time-consuming and it has no sure guarantee of a victorious ending. Yet as long as human history continues, autonomy will always lift its head under any circumstances in the name of the depth of reason united with a theonomous ground to protect man from the comeback of old superstitions, the creations of new enslaving codes, and to supply him with vision, tenacity, and strength to wait upon the descendence of a kairos moment in each epoch.[52]

Tillich declared that one of the common meeting grounds for heteronomy and autonomy is in the totally exhausted and empty autonomy. Taking his clue from the historical fact that whenever and wherever autonomous culture becomes secular and runs out of its steam, it is heteronomy that comes in to fill the gap. In "The Present Theological Situation in the Light of the Continental Development" in *Theology Today*, he related the development of Neo-Protestantism as indicative of the fact that "autonomy inescapably becomes secular, producing an empty space into which demonic heteronomies enter."[53] Note the plural form Tillich used with regard to heteronomy here. It is in line with his rational deduction based on thoroughgoing historical and experiential analyses that when heteronomy descends upon man it is usually in more than one sphere of life that the exercise of its powers is extended to. A heteronomy might take footrest on the religious sphere first but gradually yet steadily its impact will be felt in other dimensions of life such as art, politics, or morality, driving the remainder of autonomous elements further into exile—into a no-man's land ultimately.

If one is to narrow his horizon to the relationship between heteronomy and human reason he will note that the former imposes an alien law on at least one and frequently on all of the functions of the latter. It dispatches its orders from 'outside' on how reason should behave in grasping and shaping reality. But this 'outside' is not exactly outside, so Tillich's argument goes. It represents at the same time an element in reason itself, namely, the depth of reason. Therefore, a conflict between heteronomy and autonomy is a conflict in reason itself. The problem of heteronomy is a problem of an authority which claims to represent reason, that is, the depth of reason, against its autonomous actu-

---

[52] See "Beyond Religious Socialism," *The Christian Century*, June 15, 1949, p. 733.

[53] "The Present Theological Situation in the Light of the Continental Development," *Theology Today*, October, 1949, p. 307.

alization. Tillich speculated that the basis of a genuine heteronomy is the claim to speak in behalf of the ground of being and therefore in an unconditional way. A heteronomous authority usually takes its form of expression in terms of myth and cult because these are the direct expressions of the depth of reason. Heteronomy in this sense is in most cases a reaction against an autonomy which has lost its depth and has become empty and a misfit which has exhausted its usefulness. But of course as a reaction it is destructive, denying reason the right to autonomy and destroying its structural laws from outside.[54]

The discussion on the interrelationships between heteronomy and theonomy unavoidably involves frequent reference to autonomy also and it is in this context that this last portion of the present subsection is dealt with.

To discern the difference between heteronomy and theonomy is simultaneously to detect the affinity between them. The point that must be taken into consideration is the question of authority which both theonomy and heteronomy claim to possess—although in a divergent way. Their basic difference in viewpoints with regard to the source and the validity of authority lies simply in this fact: while heteronomy claims its authority to be inherent in itself, theonomy bases its authority on the absolute, the ultimate, the being-itself. A case in point is Jesus' utterance in the Fourth Gospel in connection with the disciples' belief in him: He that believeth on me, believeth not on me, but on him that sent me.[55] What makes Jesus the Christ and the New Being is his ever-present and never-ceasing efforts to point to him from whom all human beings come and to whom they must return and therefore must face with ultimate concern. None other is more justified than Jesus himself to claim infinite loyalty from people and yet all through his life he made it his lifework to call people to focus their hearts, minds, and souls on the ground of all beings, their heavenly Father, the source of all authorities and life. A theonomous authority is one that is united with courage and creativity in the depth of soul whereas a heteronomous authority lies in its suppressive power with its tendency to regard and make itself an absolute.[56]

In theonomy, the divine being transforms all the preliminary author-ities into media of himself. The parental authority, the authority of

---

[54] *ST I*, pp. 84f.
[55] The Gospel of St. John 12: 44.
[56] See "The Protestant Vision," *The Chicago Theological Seminary Register*, March, 1950, p. 10.

earthly wisdom and human knowledge, the authorities of the communities and society, the authority of the church, even the authority of Jesus the Christ as a bearer of the New Being are all changed into God's tools to make his will shine through and thereby to create a theonomy in an individual, a community, or an age. Within this theonomous realm, everything can become a medium of revelation, a bearer of divine power. By 'everything' is meant

> all things in nature and culture, in soul and history; it also includes principles, categories, essences, and values. Through stars and stones, trees and animals, growth and catastrophe; through tools and houses, sculpture and melody, poems and prose, laws and customs (that are commonly the authoritative tools for heteronomy); through parts of the body and functions of the mind, family relations and voluntary communities, historical leaders and national elevation; through time and space, being and nonbeing, ideas and virtues, the holy can encounter us.[57]

Tillich concluded that autonomy and heteronomy are both rooted in theonomy and each goes astray when their theonomous unity is broken. It can be clearly seen that theonomous elements can come in conflict with an autonomous heteronomy, for example, in ecclesiastical or political provenience, and in that situation the autonomous elements in it can be defeated and temporarily suppressed. However, the fact of a permanent struggle between autonomous independence and heteronomous reaction, or heteronomous suppression and autonomous reaction, leads to the quest for a new theonomy. Revelation overcomes the conflict between autonomy and heteronomy by reestablishing their essential unity. A perfect theonomy keeps autonomous reason from losing its depth and from becoming empty and open to demonic intrusions and, on the other hand, keeps heteronomous reason from establishing itself against rational autonomy or to engross theonomy in the process of the exercise of its authorities.[58]

---

[57] *Biblical Religion and the Search for Ultimate Reality*, pp. 22f. See also "By What Authority?," *The New Being*, pp. 79-91.
[58] *ST I*, pp. 85 and 147. Compare also with *ST III*, pp. 250ff.

CHAPTER V

The Pedagogical Principles of Christian Education

The structure of the next two chapters is as follows: Chapter V, Section I. General Characteristics of Three Theologically Distinctive Groups. Section II. The Pedagogical Principles of Conservative Christian Educators. Under Chapter VI, Section III. The Pedagogical Principles of Liberal Christian Educators. Section IV. The Pedagogical Principles of Reconstructed Liberal Christian Educators.

I. GENERAL CHARACTERISTICS OF THREE THEOLOGICALLY DISTINCTIVE GROUPS

In dealing with the pedagogical principles[1] of Christian education, three theologically distinctive groups in the Protestant church are examined through the writings of major spokesmen. After consultation with the members of the faculty of the Department of Religious Education, New York University, this researcher adopted the nine leading religious educators named below, who are classified according to their theological orientations.[2]

Conservatives: Frank E. Gaebelein and Lois E. LeBar

Liberals: George A. Coe, Harrison S. Elliot, and Sophia L. Fahs

---

[1] Note: "Pedagogical principle" is here interpreted simply as "the fundamental law of the theory of how to teach." See *Webster's New International Dictionary*, p. 1589 and *Standard Dictionary of the English Language*, p. 929. Referral is also made to *The Oxford English Dictionary*, p. 1376 and *Webster's Seventh New Collegiate Dictionary*, p. 676.

[2] Note: Same classification of religious educators under these categories was made by Norma H. Thompson, now an Associate Professor of the said department, and Walter Nyberg, University of the Pacific, California, in their doctoral dissertations.

Reconstructed Liberals: Iris V. Cully, Randolph C. Miller, Lewis
   J. Sherrill, and D. Campbell Wyckoff

These religious educators were chosen because (1) of their recognized eminence in the field, (2) all of them hold or held degrees in religious education from leading universities or seminaries in the United States, (3) they have spent most of their lives in the schools or seminaries where Christian educators are trained, (4) they have contributed extensively through books, essays, and articles to the literature in the field, (5) their published works were accessible to this investigator.

It seems necessary that before an attempt is made to determine, evaluate, and compare the pedagogical principles explicitly adhered to, or implicitly assumed, by these nine religious educators,[3] the writer should present the characteristics of each of the three named groups in Protestant Christian education. These characteristics constitute the background materials for utilizing the findings of the preceding and following chapters. These materials are drawn primarily from articles in *The Westminster Dictionary of Christian Education,* published in 1963 and edited by Kendig B. Cully, now Dean of the New York Theological Seminary in New York City. This dictionary was chosen because it is (1) edited by one of the leading religious educators of this generation, (2) the first dictionary of its kind ever published—a comprehensive work with religious education as its primary focus, (3) international in scope and interdenominational in content, as can be seen from the list of its contributors, (4) a volume wherein all the contributors are authorities in their respective fields, and (5) one in which the spokesmen in all three categories adopted on pages 56-57 are included.

Conservatives in Christian Education

Conservatism is both a movement in the history of the Christian church and a doctrinal system, and an understanding of the former will help to clarify the spirit of conservatism.

Dismayed by "the employment of the scientific method of inquiry, higher criticism in the study of the Scriptures, and the popularization of the evolutionary hypothesis"[4] adhered to by the liberal Christians, some Protestants felt that their faith was being undermined and they became, at the beginning of the twentieth century, devoted to the refutation of liberalism.

---

[3] For their written works, see pages 124-125.
[4] *The Westminster Dictionary of Christian Education,* p. 271.

The publication in 1909 of 12 paperback books under the series title, *The Fundamentals*, which was distributed free to pastors, evangelists, missionaries, seminary professors and students, Y.M.C.A. and Y.W.C.A. secretaries, college professors, Sunday school superintendents, and religious editors throughout the English-speaking world, incited widespread controversy and led to the formation of a theologically distinctive group within Christendom, namely, fundamentalists, who are in this study equated with the conservatives.

As consequences of these factors and as seminaries, literature, and missionary agencies began to feel the impact of liberalism, various actions began within denominations. Conservative Northern Baptist Theological Seminary was founded in 1913 as a protest against liberalism in the Divinity School of the University of Chicago. Likewise, the Westminster Theological Seminary was established in Philadelphia as a protest against what some saw as the encroaching menace found in the liberal Princeton Theological Seminary in New Jersey.

The conservatives in the Christian church are generally known as those who believe in and hold strong "allegiance to the basic truths of Scripture," and who firmly believe in certain articles of faith, some of which are: (1) the authority and infallibility of the Bible; (2) the Trinity; (3) the deity, virgin birth, substitutionary death, bodily resurrection, ascension, and return of Jesus Christ; (4) regeneration by the Holy Spirit; (5) indwelling of the Holy Spirit in the believer; (6) resurrection of all men—the saved unto life eternal, the lost unto eternal damnation; and (7) the spiritual unity of all believers.[5]

Adherence to doctrinal statements sometimes becomes for conservatives a test of fellowship, and in some groups there are strict standards of conduct. The marks of real salvation to some conservatives have included deliverance from such alleged evils as dancing, card-playing, attending the theater, smoking, and gambling.[6] In other words, conservatives are those who submit themselves willingly to the authority of the Scriptures and, in a lesser degree, to the rule of certain creeds, articles of faith, doctrinal statements, or strict standards of conduct.[7]

It must be noted that in very recent years an extreme Biblical lit-

---

[5] *Ibid.*, p. 272.

[6] *Ibid.*

[7] Note: See the Bulletin of Wheaton College, Wheaton, Illinois, 1962-1963, *Standards of Conduct*, pp. 10-11. Also, the Bulletin of Fuller Theological Seminary, Pasadena, California, 1961-1962, *Purpose*, p. 8 and the *Statement of Faith*, pp. 9-10. These institutions are good representatives of conservative, or evangelical, Christian schools on college and seminary levels.

eralism among conservatives is much less prominent in curriculum materials and in some instances memorization is de-emphasized. There appears to be more concern that all the pupils and students in the conservative camp engage in a systematic study of the Bible with definite application to the questions and problems of daily life.

Liberals in Christian Education

In sharp contrast to the conservatives, liberals are those who believe in the use of the scientific method of inquiry, historical and textual criticisms in the study of the Scriptures, and the basic hypotheses of the evolutionary theory. They adhere "to freedom from prior commitments (save those to the liberal spirit), and to the willingness to break through present structures of thought or practice in order to formulate new patterns."[8]

The method acceptable to the liberals is that of science: the empirical, inductive process by which anything—any law, any common belief, any human experience—may be explored in the quest for knowledge or in the exposing of old falsehoods. Understandably, they reject vehemently the old views of authority, "building their doctrines on religious experience and on rational-empirical grounds."[9]

The cardinal affirmation of liberalism is "the infinite dignity and value of man as man," for "anthropology is the heart of the system." Some other marks of liberalism are: (1) the teaching of the continuity of the divine being with his creation marks the stress on God's immanence. The picture the liberals draw of God is copied to the greatest extent from the Gospels' portrait of Jesus. The liberals use a process called "Christologizing," thereby gradually losing sight of God as transcendental judge and king and reducing him to a kind Father; (2) the portrayal of Jesus Christ, the Son of God, more in terms of his humanity than of his divinity; as the prototype of man at his highest and best—as one who has fully realized the potential within. Attaining "Christlikeness" becomes for liberals the goal of religious practice and discipleship training; (3) Christianity tends to be defined by liberals as an ethical religion or at least primarily of such a nature. The core of Christian life is manifested in the declaration: "The brotherhood of man under the Fatherhood of God." Love is to be expressed in terms of the struggle for social justice through reconstruction of the forms of

---

[8] The Westminster Dictionary of Christian Education, op. cit., p. 390.
[9] Ibid., p. 461.

the social system; (4) the church is regarded by liberals as nothing unique in its origin, nature, and function. The church is seen largely as an institution of society devoted to the betterment of character and social structure; (5) the Bible stands as a book among many holy scriptures of religion, full of wisdom and guidance for men to utilize in their lives. It also demonstrates the progressive development of men's religious consciousness and perception as they came to know more and more of God and his purposes by reflecting upon their experiences; and (6) man is saved not by sudden conversion upon conviction of his sin but by gradual growth in knowledge and maturity.[10]

During the first forty years of this century, most of the creative and influential leaders in Christian education were possessors of the liberal spirit and adherents of these liberal doctrines and beliefs. They taught the doctrine of irreversible gradual progression toward individual and social perfection in the world. The catastrophes and inhumanity witnessed in two World Wars shattered the liberals' conviction so extensively, however, that by the early 1950s many individuals and groups within the liberal camp were hard at work reassessing their basic beliefs and reconstructing new ones.

Reconstructed Liberals in Christian Education

The reconstructed liberals stress both the "revealed character of the Christian faith . . . (and) the place of reason in determining the substance of Christian belief." They insist that reason must be relied upon "to receive revelation, to distinguish between true and false revelation claims, to interpret the implications of revelation for living and to establish bridges of understanding for communication of the revealed truth to many kinds of people."[11]

The reconstructed liberals, although emphasizing more than the majority of the liberals the uniqueness of the Christian message and the vital importance of the Holy Scriptures, nevertheless insist that God has also disclosed himself and much truth among men of other traditions. They believe, moreover, that the Bible itself supports this view.[12]

The reconstructed liberals freely grant that some theology of the last century, especially under the influence of Schleiermacher, so stressed the immanence of God as to lose sight of his mysterious and awesome transcendence. They agree that God is transcendent beyond all human

[10] *Ibid.*, p. 391.
[11] *Ibid.*, p. 460.
[12] See Romans chapters 1 and 2; and Acts 14: 16-17.

imagination or comprehension. Yet they insist that he is immanent also. "He is radically other than man, but also deeply concerned with man and continuously active in the world." Some liberals have come close to identifying the Kingdom of God with human accomplishments of reform or certain social institutions. The reconstructed liberals emphatically deny such identification. Yet they insist that the Kingdom of God is God's reigning in human hearts, wills, and relationships. "Its coming depends on God, but also upon the faithful obedience of men in subjecting all human experience, institutions, and relationships to his rule."[13]

Obviously the limits of reconstructed liberalism cannot be defined with precision. But Roger L. Shinn of the Union Theological Seminary in New York writes that:

> Any appraisal of contemporary theology must note the renewed interest in traditional doctrines once widely regarded as passe. Thus theology appeals often to Biblical revelation, to the transcendence of God, to the awareness of human sin, to Jesus Christ as the revelation and deed of God, to recognition of tragedy in history, to an eschatological hope.[14]

These emphases echo the themes of the Bible, particularly of Saint Paul's writings, of Augustine, and of the Protestant reformers such as Martin Luther and John Calvin.

But reconstructed liberalism likewise owes much to the "liberal" elements within it. Roger L. Shinn continues to state:

> It looks to science rather than Scripture for the description of cosmic processes. It often takes Biblical doctrines (e.g., of the Fall of man and the resurrection of the body) 'seriously but not literally,' in Niebuhr's well-known phrase. It recognizes the relativism of all human thinking, including creeds and theologies.[15]

Particularly in the United States of America, it appeals not to the infallible authority of the Bible but to a Biblical interpretation of experience.

In summary, reconstructed liberals are those who endeavor to maintain a reasonable balance by simultaneously preserving the strengths and rejecting the weaknesses of both conservative and liberal groups. They are among those who are "quite open to all scientific findings,"

---

13 *The Westminster Dictionary of Christian Education*, op. cit., p. 460.
14 *Ibid.*, p. 463.
15 *Ibid.*

but make "a sharp distinction between Christian faith and the prevailing spirit of modern culture."[16]

II. The Pedagogical Principles of Conservative Christian Educators

In his effort to discover the pedagogical principles adhered to, or implicitly assumed, by spokesmen of the conservative group for the purpose of (1) comparing them with the pedagogical principles adhered to by the representatives of liberal and reconstructed liberal groups and (2) finding their compatibility, or proving their incompatibility, with Paul Tillich's concepts of theonomy, autonomy, and heteronomy, this researcher has deliberately divided this section into two subsections, the methodology of which will be followed also in the sections in the next chapter. They are: A. Implicit Statements on Pedagogical Principles made by these spokesmen. B. Explicit Statements on Teaching Methods. The contents in these two chapters are drawn exclusively from the primary sources listed on pages 124-125 in the Bibliography.

A. Implicit Statements on Pedagogical Principles

1. Discovery of God's Ways

Both LeBar and Gaebelein make the point that, consciously or unconsciously, some kind of method is always involved in an act of teaching, irrespective of the form of teaching it takes.[17] LeBar, in verifying this point, calls attention to the pedagogical principles inherent in Saint Paul's teaching in the forms of sermons and letters.[18]

Both LeBar and Gaebelein are of the opinion that, as far as teaching method is concerned, the real task in Christian education is to discover God's ways by the work of the Holy Spirit and to work with rather than against him.[19] Because they are God's ways and can be known only through the inspiration of the Holy Spirit, these methods contain divine qualities, although they are shown to and comprehended by human instructors. The transcendent qualities of divine methods, though simple rather than complicated, are derived from the fact that they require

---

[16] *Ibid.*, p. 462.
[17] Lois E. LeBar, *Education That Is Christian*, p. 16. See also Frank E. Gaebelein, *Christian Education in a Democracy*, p. 113.
[18] LeBar, *Ibid.*, p. 87.
[19] *Ibid.*, p. 241. Also pp. 136, 230, and 232. And Gaebelein, *op. cit.*, p. 248.

spiritual insight into the nature of God, the nature of man, the purpose of the Scriptures, and the means of getting pupils into the written Word and through the Book to the living Word in Jesus Christ.[20]

2. Belief Is a Key

In order that one may discover God's ways of teaching and his ways of dealing with man, one must, as a necessary prerequisite, possess the mind and heart to trust in God, believe in Christ, and commit oneself wholly to the teaching of the Holy Scriptures. Faith over reason, and supernatural enlightenment, take precedence over critical, human search in this enterprise.[21]

This commitment of the whole person—body, mind, and spirit—to God in Christ, Gaebelein claims, is not only a prerequisite and indispensable condition in learning God's ways, but it is also the final goal of Christian education.[22]

3. The Bi-polarity of Christ and the Bible

It is not an overstatement to say that the theological basis—as well as the theological foundation in Christian education—of conservatives is bi-polar: it is rooted solidly and equally on both sovereignty of God in Christ Jesus and inerrant authority of the Holy Scriptures.[23] Some of the explicit statements made by LeBar and Gaebelein support this point.

"The center of Christian education," Gaebelein writes, "is the One whom God has sent." He continues his proclamation on the centrality of Christ with the following statement: "What is the factor that distinguishes a Christian philosophy of education from other religious philosophies, such as Judaism or a theistic view based on Greek thought? It is this one thing—the centrality of Jesus Christ."[24]

Moving over to the other pole of this double-emphasis, one notes that on the opening pages of his book, *Christian Education for a Democracy*, Gaebelein forcefully urges Christian education to be recalled to the path from which it wandered long ago. He suggests all Christians should grant that "the path is an old one, that it is based upon certain

---

[20] LeBar, *Ibid.*, p. 5.

[21] Gaebelein, *op. cit.*, pp. 30, 44, and 161.

[22] *Ibid.*, pp. 36, 227, and 229.

[23] See LeBar, *op. cit.*, pp. 169 and 224; also Gaebelein, *The Pattern of God's Truth*, pp. 22 and 66.

[24] Gaebelein, *Christian Education in a Democracy*, pp. 33 and 25, respectively.

great truths found in full power only in the Bible," and that "the only criterion for the path (Christian) education must take is neither popularity nor 'modernity,' but eternal truth" found in the written Word of God.[25]

Relating the place of Scriptures to the curriculum of Christian education, Gaebelein answers the question: What place should the Bible have in a Christian school? There is only one logical answer possible, he avers: "It must have the first place. Here we are drawn to use a familiar educational term and to say that 'the core curriculum' of any system of Christian education must be Biblical."[26] To Gaebelein, the centrality of the Bible in Christian education is organic. It not only provides a unifying frame of reference for every other subject; it also gives life and power to the whole curriculum.

4. Authoritarian Method Rejected

Since conservatives are those who generally adhere and willingly submit to certain authorities, be it the Bible, Christ, doctrines, creeds, or standards of conduct, one might naturally be under the impression that they still retain rote method with indoctrination of certain creeds, doctrines, or Biblical passages as their primary aim. This is far from the truth. Both LeBar and Gaebelein vehemently reject authoritarian, or transmissive, or rote method in the conservative's teaching in schools, colleges, and the other teaching-learning organizations of their camp.[27] LeBar points out specifically a mistake made by many of those who stand outside the conservative camp in identifying authoritative message within its walls with authoritarian method still employed in some corners in the field of religious education, her own group included.[28]

5. Insights of Other Fields Utilized

What the conservatives adhere to as far as teaching method is concerned is to utilize all means, ways, and fields of learning as doors to God's methods, in the process adapting and adjusting to all the insights used not only by related fields of studies such as educational psychology, history and philosophy of education, and the problems of higher edu-

---

25 *Ibid.*, p. 8. Compare with *The Pattern of God's Truth*, p. 31.
26 *Ibid.*, pp. 119f.
27 LeBar, *op. cit.*, pp. 28f; and Gaebelein, *Ibid.*, p. 162.
28 LeBar, *Ibid.*, p. 171.

cation[29] but also by God's truth in Scripture, in nature, in science, literature, art, and in all of life.[30] Gaebelein thus expresses:

> We do indeed give primacy to that spiritual truth revealed in the Bible and incarnate in Christ. That does not mean, however, that those aspects of truth discoverable by man in the realm of mathematics, chemistry, or geography, are any whit less God's truth than the truth as it is in Christ. The difference is clearly a question of subject matter. In the latter case, the subject matter is of a different importance from the former; truth about Christ pertains to salvation, that about physics does not . . . But all the time there is the unity of all truth under God, and that unity we deny in education at the peril of habituating ourselves to the fragmentary kind of learning found on some avowedly Christian campuses today.[31]

In fact, 'all truths are God's truth' is the main theme around which Gaebelein centripetally developed his chapters in the book, *The Pattern of God's Truth*, published in 1954.

B. Explicit Statements on Teaching Methods

1. Experience Emphasized

Contrary to the general impression, one is immensely surprised by the abundance of references in which conservatives emphasize the importance of the role of experience in the business of teaching as well as of learning. Both LeBar and Gaebelein make it clear beyond any doubt that their pedagogy is founded on experience-centered method. To hear Gaebelein speak again:

> It is a valid principle in education that students learn by doing. Therefore, the need for training is of highest importance. Required chapel, yes. But woe to the school that does not balance this with carefully planned opportunities for voluntary participation in religious activities.[32]

---

[29] Gaebelein, *Christian Education in a Democracy*, p. 204.

[30] Gaebelein, *The Pattern of God's Truth*, pp. 20, 23, and 107; also *Christian Education in a Democracy*, p. 30.

[31] *Ibid.*, pp. 22f. See also *Christian Education in a Democracy*, pp. 34 and 48. In the latter, on page 48, Gaebelein quotes from John 1: 3, Colossians 1: 17, 2: 3, and Hebrews 1: 2-3 to verify the point that all studies are indeed sacred because everything was made and is upheld by the Creator.

[32] Gaebelein, *Christian Education in a Democracy*, p. 59.

"After all," Gaebelein goes on, "the problem of religious education can be understood only in the framework of education in general. And education may be broadly described as the changing of human beings through experience."[33] He iterates that the Bible knows no such thing as truth that is merely theoretical; in the Bible truth is linked to the deed. This principle is witnessed in its highest expression, so Gaebelein says, in the atonement in the life and work of Jesus Christ.[34] He is the eternal Word of God, logos, incarnate—living and working among mankind.

To LeBar, the peculiar genius of teaching is found in a small intimate group in which overt interaction is possible.[35] One of the major tasks of a teacher is to "set up situations for the practice of sharing, working together," and also to provide opportunities according to pupils' capacities and needs. Teaching as well as learning is, for LeBar, an inner process on the pupil's part.[36]

By emphasizing experience as a prime factor in the teaching-and-learning enterprise, the conservatives lay stress also on the pupil-centered approach in their pedagogy. This means that the selection of all materials, Biblical or otherwise, must be suitable to the needs and capacities of the pupil, and the pupil must be the center around which the selection, arrangement, procedure, and conclusion are premeditated. The teacher must project himself into the place of his pupils, and try to feel as they feel, think as they think, walk in their shoes. Then teaching becomes a great adventure with the Master Teacher himself.[37]

2. Faith Plus Reason

To adhere to a pupil-centered approach means, among other things, to tap the pupils' rational capacities and their intellectual potentialities. Citing Jesus the Teacher, Gaebelein writes that "although He emphasized the centrality of faith, He also taught His disciples to think for themselves. The Gospels contain no record of Christ's rebuking an honest inquirer."[38] This attitude as a teacher was followed not only by Saint Paul but by Saint Augustine, Martin Luther, John Calvin, Jona-

---

[33] *Ibid.*, p. 67.
[34] Gaebelein, *The Pattern of God's Truth*, p. 35.
[35] LeBar, *Education that Is Christian*, p. 21.
[36] *Ibid.*, pp. 143f. See also pp. 34-37, where she cites Jean Rousseau, Johann Pestalozzi, Friedrich Froebel and John Dewey to implement her point.
[37] LeBar, *op. cit.*, p. 138. See also p. 148.
[38] Gaebelein, *Christian Education in a Democracy*, p. 202.

than Edwards, John Wesley, and others. God likes to find and then cultivate consecrated intellect in all men.[39]

Although it is correct to state that the common consensus of conservatives is that they believe in the revealed truth, their approach to education is by way of revelation plus reason. In approaching and in discovering new aspects of God's truth, man's reason plays, under the guidance of the spirit of God, a necessary part. Though on its highest level God's truth is received by faith, it can also be known through reason, enlightened by the Holy Spirit.[40]

3. Outer Plus Inner Factors

LeBar makes a unique contribution to the pedagogical principles of Christian education among evangelicals by iterating and reiterating throughout her book, *Education That Is Christian*, what she designates as a balance between outer and inner factors. By outer factors, she means the curriculum, the lessons, and Biblical or doctrinal contents that must be taught from outside; by inner, the volition, the initiative, and the comprehension on and from the pupil's part. To her, a perfect balance and equilibrium between those two factors in the teaching process in Christian education constitutes a theonomous methodology. She cites a perfect embodiment of this pedagogical principle and practice in Jesus' own. By working with the Holy Spirit and letting the Holy Spirit work through the living Word, namely himself, Jesus made the outer Word an inner experience in his encounters with the Samaritan woman;[41] Nichodemus;[42] the blind men;[43] and in the parables by the sea.[44]

For LeBar, Jesus usually started on a personal level because then the pupils were able to correlate their own life experiences with his eternal truth. In a few times when Jesus started on a content level,[45] he continually related that content to the lives of his hearers. From the synoptic study of the Gospels, it must be acknowledged that in most of Jesus' teaching situations outer factors were balanced by inner.

Even before Jesus' time, LeBar points out, the education that the

---

[39] ————, *The Pattern of God's Truth*, p. 105.

[40] *Ibid.*, p. 29.

[41] LeBar, *Education That Is Christian*, pp. 52-58. Read John 4: 1-41.

[42] *Ibid.*, pp. 59-62. And John 3: 1-13.

[43] *Ibid.*, pp. 62-69. Read Matthew 9: 27-34, Mark 8: 22-26, John 9. Also Matthew 20: 29-34, Mark 10: 46-52, and Luke 18: 35-43.

[44] *Ibid.*, pp. 69-72. Compare with Matthew 13: 1-52, Mark 4: 1-34, and Luke 8: 4-18.

[45] For example, in Nichodemus' case.

Lord God gave the Jewish people whom he had chosen for his own purposes was theocentric and practical, with a solutary balance between inner and outer factors. "He taught them by precept and example, by knowing and doing, by questions and moral discipline, memorization and sensory appeal . . . Knowing, feeling, and doing were balanced in doctrine, worship, and holy living."[46]

Condemning and rejecting both the purely Bible-centered curriculum and the secular and religious liberal curriculum with its emphasis on experience alone, LeBar advocates an approach of the human teacher working along with the divine Teacher toward an amalgamation of inner and outer forces so that it is difficult to separate them.[47]

4. Creative Christian Education

Gaebelein teaches specifically from the evangelical point of view by stating that religious education is: (a) the transmission by the Christian church or the Christian community of the Judaeo-Christian heritage, including the Bible as the record of God's will and his plan for man's redemption centering in the sacrificial gift of Jesus Christ; (b) the application of the specific teachings of the Bible to life and conduct, including the individual's relationships in society; (c) training in the approach to God through Christian worship; (d) directing the student to that transforming experience which comes only from personal contact by faith with Christ as Lord and Savior; and (e) leading the student on through continuing nurture to increasing stature in Christian character.[48]

LeBar supplements Gaebelein's view by discussing in great detail what she calls 'Creative Christian Teaching.' She maintains that true Christian teaching is by its very nature creative. All Christian teachers and professors must try to relate the unchanging Word to people who are always changing. She has six points which spell out how and what creative Christian teaching should be. A summarized form of these six points follows:

(1) The first step in Christian teaching is for the teacher to prepare himself spiritually.
(2) If the teacher ponders several possibilities, he will be freer than otherwise to follow the lead of the pupils.

---

[46] LeBar, op. cit., p. 27.
[47] Ibid., pp. 204-207.
[48] Gaebelein, Christian Education in a Democracy, pp. 71f.

(3) Because pupils are full of surprises, the teacher should always be ready to shift gears, moving flexibly toward the goals.

(4) Though Christian content is authoritative, the pupils themselves determine the selection of content, its order, speed, and details.

(5) The spirit helps the teacher determine when to declare truth and when to guide the pupils in discovering the truth for themselves. Because it is usually easier and more natural for the teacher to declare, he should take pains to perfect the art of guidance.

(6) A variety of methods suggest themselves as the teacher seeks to help the pupils make the outer spiritual factors their own. He should be constantly using new combinations of methods—drawings, models, illustrations of principles, posters, maps, creative writing of prose and poetry, discussion, role playing, skits, debate, reports, composing music, adapting music, games, tests, interviews, research, trips, observations, collections, time lines, planning worship services, choral reading, etc.[49]

5. Findings of Other Disciplines Utilized

Gaebelein makes it plain that the insights gained by philsophers or philosophers of education must be utilized in full in application to teaching methods in Christian education. The best way in which the Scriptural lessons can be conveyed to pupils is, according to this author, to adopt Whitehead's 'The Rhythm of Education,' by which he meant "that different subjects and modes of study should be undertaken by pupils at fitting times when they have reached the proper stage of mental development." To Whitehead, the rhythm of education consists of a continuous repetition of three cycles: "the stage of romance," "the stage of precision," and "the stage of generalization." Quoting from Whitehead, Gaebelein writes thus:

> The stage of romance is 'a process of discovery . . . dominated by wonder'; the stage of precision is controlled by 'the inescapable fact that there are right ways and wrong ways, and definite truths to be known' and holds 'that the only discipline, important for its own sake, is self-discipline'; and the stage of generalization is a return, but with a mind which is now 'a disciplined regiment instead of a rabble,' 'to the stage of romance, a reversion to discovery and initiative.'[50]

---

[49] Read LeBar, op. cit., pp. 196-201.

[50] Gaebelein, Christian Education in a Democracy, p. 122. Also read Whitehead, Ibid., pp. 25-48.

6. Methodology as Yet to Be Explored

Conservatives do not pretend to have acquired all the know-hows and answers to the question of pedagogy in Christian education. In fact, they, particularly Gaebelein, repeatedly insist that much has yet to be learned and studied on this subject. To quote him once again: "To criticize, evaluate, and then apply, in so far as they are true, such insights as those of Whitehead to the use of the Bible is a challenge which, when accepted by dedicated Christian thought, will open up new avenues in evangelical pedagogy."[51] It is bad enough for a secular subject, say English literature, to be taught poorly because such pedagogical malpractice can do life-long damage to cultural growth. But to teach the Bible or related subjects poorly is vastly worse because the nurture of the soul is at stake. Yet the most urgent call in schools and colleges given over to the evangelical faith is for better teaching methods. On this, much has yet to be learned, particularly on a college level. Gaebelein sounds alarm. Says he, "No college . . . can rest its academic oars; it must strive through constant study and revision of methods and courses to keep abreast of the times."[52]

Near the end of the book, *Christian Education in a Demoracy*, the author pointedly and sharply states: There is one field in particular wherein much pioneer work must be done, namely, methodology. Comparatively little has as yet been accomplished in the interpretation of methods of teaching and Biblical principles . . . It will demand the formulation of alternative principles at points where present-day theory is incompatible with revealed truth. And it will take careful investigation based on classroom use to determine methods that combine fidelity to Scriptures and genuine practicality.[53]

---

[51] *Ibid.*, p. 123.
[52] *Ibid.*, p. 151. See also pp. 121 and 147.
[53] *Ibid.*, p. 284.

CHAPTER VI

The Pedagogical Principles of Christian Education—(*Continued*)

III. THE PEDAGOGICAL PRINCIPLES OF LIBERAL CHRISTIAN EDUCATION

Before examining the pedagogical principles of the liberal group, several points must summarily be presented as an introduction.

First, one of the major characteristics of the liberal group is the primary role liberal religious educators place on the method of inquiry in teaching. As was stated earlier,[1] the liberals, since the turn of the century, believe in the employment of the scientific method of inquiry, higher criticism in the study of the Scriptures, and the freedom to break away from prior commitment, thereby creating something new. Second, the liberals believe that the source of basic conflicts on the religious scene has been the factor of confidence in man and of the scientific attitude which originated in the period of Enlightenment. Thus "empirical data and educational insights rather than theological concepts have been the controlling factor in the development of problem and method in religious education."[2] Third, another conviction that controls the liberal's thinking, in so far as teaching methods are concerned, is that these are not static tools but are living and moving parts of the collective life, and their improvements are all to the good.[3] Finally, technique, as defined by Coe, includes, in addition to instruction which aims to increase the pupil's knowledge, "opening the world of religious appreciation, the induction of self-discipline, the enlargement of purposes, and the development of judgment and initiative." Further, where-

---

[1] See page 118.

[2] Harrison S. Elliot, *Can Religious Education Be Christian?*, p. 4.

[3] George A. Coe, *A Social Theory of Religious Education*, viii and p. 15.

as technique is assumed by many to be merely instrumental and external to the thing that is to be transmitted, it properly is "the sensitive and foresighted response of the teacher to the movements of the pupil's personality." Thus understood, Coe continued, technique is as spiritual as anything in the content of learning can possibly be. "It is spirituality in action here and now. But—and here is the crux of the matter—it makes the pupils and the teacher co-agents with the content in determining what is to be."[4]

A.   Implicit Statements on Pedagogical Principles

1. Imposition Theory Rejected

Outrightly, both Coe and Elliot rejected the authoritarian, imposition theory in Christian teaching. Coe bluntly stated that imposition of the teacher's interpretation, views, and beliefs is contrary to genuine teaching.[5] In fact, he rejected even the "overemphasis upon the personality of the teacher, and the resort to beguilements, persuasions, and emotional pressure to induce pupils to be religious." "We are just now reacting against two types of religious work with them (children)," he went on, naming them to be "the formal or catechetical-type, and the revival or conversation-experience type."[6]

Evidence reveals that both Coe and Elliot did not hesitate at all in pointing their fingers at the imposition or transmitive approach to Christian pedagogy as one of the main reasons why things had not gone right in the field. Elliot stated in effect: Evidently the emphases upon education as a method of training children and young people in the accepted adult beliefs and practices are in part responsible for the failure of religious education in the past to result in fundamental improvement of individual and corporate life.[7]

The best embodiment and example of such authoritarian method is found in his time in Roman Catholicism, according to Coe. In his book, A Social Theory of Christian Education, Coe analyzed the Roman Catholic Church's theory in minute detail. He summarized the "Presupposition of Roman Catholic education" as follows:

---

[4] Coe, What Is Christian Education?, pp. 19 and 54, respectively.

[5] Read Ibid., pp. 210f. Compare with Elliot, op. cit., p. 13.

[6] Coe, A Social Theory of Christian Education, pp. 97 and 140, respectively. See also p. 28.

[7] Elliot, op. cit., pp. 225f. Compare with Coe, What Is Christian Education?, pp. 35 and 41.

(1) Education is the transmission of a completed faith, not participation in the evolution of a faith. Repetition, reproduction, prevention of change within the scope of religion—this rather than experiment, new enterprise, or discovery, is the spirit.

(2) The basal process in this transmission is intellectualistic.

(3) Both dogma and rules of conduct are to be imposed upon the pupil by authority. This authority, moreover, is lodged in living men who announce and administer penalties for nonconformity. Authority as teacher, authority to command what is to be believed and done, descends in orderly gradation from the Pope to every priest.

Speaking on "The fundamentals of method in Roman Catholic education," Coe wrote that "it is not by any subtle trick, or ingenious device, or mysterious influence that Catholicism secures these results, but by the persistent and organized use of simple and obvious methods" that they attain their aims in education. They are:

(1) Habit-formation by drill processes is the pervading essence of the whole (enterprise) . . . Conscience, taste, and in fact standards of judgment in every sphere can become petrified as habits.

(2) Hence the great prominence of memory drill upon verbal formulae. Since exact conformity is the end sought, the stress is never removed from the verbal forms in which the Church has clothed her teachings. That is, habit-formation, not independent judgment, remains the essence of the method to the very end.

(3) Expression from the pupil takes the forms of reproduction of what he has been told rather than that of "free self-expression."

(4) Gradation of material, in the proper sense of "gradation" does not exist, but rather fuller and fuller treatment of the same outline, with some change from sensuous to logical modes of impression.[8]

This kind of authoritarian approach, or transmissive education, which is defined by Coe as "policies and practices that are based upon the assumption that the primary purpose of education, by which its particular processes are to be controlled and judged, is the perpetuation of an already existing culture or some part of it,"[9] is rejected by Coe because it employs either force or evasion in the interest of effectiveness, with its eyes fixed upon content, and it is slow to apprehend the forces at work that can be utilized for free exercise of the teaching-learning process.

---

[8] Coe, *A Social Theory of Christian Education*, pp. 296-302.

[9] Coe, *What Is Christian Education?*, p. 10.

2. Pupil's Freedom Respected

Liberals have quarrels with those who embrace or adhere to the authoritarian approach in pedagogical principle on the basis of the existence—or the lack of it—of freedom. By this is meant particularly freedom on the part of the pupil. Writing on the topic of "educational tendencies of liberalism," Coe defined religious liberalism, with which he unabashedly identified himself, as "the attempt to incorporate freedom into religion. Not freedom from religion, but freedom in religion, is the idea."[10] Liberalism instills ethical principles, or teaches any subject-matter, not by authority but through reflection by inciting pupils to think for themselves. Coe mentioned three categories through which liberalism has obvious significance for a theory of religious education. They are: firstly, the effort to develop in each person an individual or independent attitude in all religious matters; secondly, the awakening of thought as contrasted with mental habituation; and thirdly, the fusion of rightness toward God with rightness toward man.[11]

The permanent elements of (1) loving approach to persons and (2) the scientific approach to facts in Christian education is not a dogma; rather it supersedes dogmatic authority, Coe said elsewhere. He continued:

> It is an attitude or a policy, and in this sense a method, or determinant and test of procedure. Further . . . it is what logicians have called a heuristic principle, that is, a way of acting that leads to discoveries. It has indefinite fecundity and creativeness because it makes us active to the limit of our personal capacity without imposing upon us any act whatever.[12]

Sophia Fahs describes in the Preface of her best known book, *Today's Children and Yesterday's Heritage*, a sharp contrast between the old philosophy of religious education and the new with the following statement: In an attempt to set forth an emerging philosophy of religious education, "we have dealt especially on those points where the natural approach to religious development stands in marked contrast to the traditional approach of authority and indoctrination." She continues to say that the changes going on that are significant are not mere methods and techniques of teaching: they cut deep into the religious beliefs and emotions of the present time.[13]

---

[10] ———, *A Social Theory of Christian Education*, p. 335.
[11] Coe, *Ibid.*, p. 336.
[12] ———, *What Is Christian Education?*, p. 179.
[13] Sophia L. Fahs, *Today's Children and Yesterday's Heritage*, Preface, vii.

74

3. Social Aspect Stressed

The foundation upon which the whole discussion was built in Coe's book, *A Social Theory of Christian Education*, was the conviction that within Protestantism there was, or was coming to be, a distinctive religious principle, that of a divine-human industrial democracy. It was based on the Biblical passage: "My father worketh hitherto, and I work."[14]

As the title of the volume reveals, Coe's intention was to construct a theory of Christian education on the basis of then widely accepted social interpretations of the Christian message. He contended that without this interpersonal aspect and social interaction the aims of religious education will not be realized. He readily acknowledged his heavy indebtedness to John Dewey, who was foremost among those who had put education and industrial democracy into a single perspective.[15]

Coe taught that in order to realize this social aim in religious education, religious instruction must intend by all means not to impose truth but to promote the growth of pupils. Hence, he recommended, the term 'instruction' must be emptied of its traditional implication of telling pupils what to believe. He expanded this point as follows:

> To impose our beliefs upon a child, even though the beliefs be utterly true, is not to promote the growth of a free personality—it may be an invasion of personality; it may subject one individual to another instead of emancipating each and every one into full membership in a self-governing society, the democracy of God.[16]

The aim of Christian education, to Coe, is then the "growth of the young toward and into mature and efficient devotion to the democracy of God, and happy self-realization therein."[17]

This does not mean that liberal Christian education is less demanding and easy-going than the authoritarian, disciplinarian type of teaching method. On the contrary, it demands stringent standards; rigorous researching; and a most intellectualistic discernment of uncertainties from certainties, the contingency of that which is contingent, and the imperfections of that which is imperfect. It would regard the problems of life not as solved but as in a process of solution that requires man to take a constant part therein. The task is truly venturesome, risky, un-

---

[14] The Gospel of John 5: 17.
[15] Coe, *A Social Theory of Christian Education*, x.
[16] *Ibid.*, pp. 64f.
[17] *Ibid.*, p. 55. See also *What Is Christian Education?*, p. 68.

predictable, and mountainously difficult. This kind of Christian education, or philosophy of religion, can never be termed a "soft pedagogy" because it is exactly the opposite of what is meant by that term. Christian education, then, is the systematic, critical examination and reconstruction of relations between persons, "guided by Jesus' assumption that persons are of infinite worth, and by the hypothesis of the existence of God, the Great Valuer of Persons."[18]

Elliot seconded Coe wholeheartedly on the social aspect of Christian education. He wrote that in any social relations the older and the younger, the more mature and the less mature, together should face the situations of life, the immature taking the initiative and the more mature furnishing protection and guidance and making resources available out of their larger experience. He continued in the following words:

> In such comradeship in meeting the situations of life in this world, human beings would be expected to take initiative, to make decisions, to take responsibility, but all the time, in relation to a God whose resources they utilize and dependence upon whom they gladly recognize. In such comradeship God becomes a living reality and at the same time man grows in the humanity as he recognizes the degree to which he is actually dependent upon God.[19]

In fact, Elliot sounded much like Coe when he stated that, "where the intelligence of individuals is enlisted in cooperative endeavor for the realization of social goals, which are the human approximation of the Kingdom of God, 'final possibilities of life' become both the incentive and the critique of every human endeavor." Further, the individual is turned from individual striving to cooperative effort. "A social and experience-centered religious education represents a process for this type of human endeavor."[20] A socialized form of religious education would seem to be of fundamental importance if God is to be dynamically and creatively experienced in human life. "The social process of religious education is the very process which gives the largest promise of bringing about a vital experience of God,"[21] Elliot concluded. The vitality of religious experience is realized only as individuals and groups are engaged in the enterprises of God on earth, and it is only in such enterprises that they can truly find a relationship to him. To Elliot, the ex-

---

[18] Coe, *What Is Christian Education?*, p. 296.

[19] Elliot, *op. cit.*, p. 160. See also pp. 159 and 209.

[20] *Ibid.*, pp. 212f. Compare with p. 226 where Elliot urged the enlistment of individuals toward the reconstruction of life of which they are a part.

[21] *Ibid.*, pp. 278f.

perience of God is integrally related to a social process of religious education.

B. Explicit Statements on Teaching Methods

1. Pupil-centered Approach

By the frequency of their strong emphases and clear statements, liberals demonstrated without any shadow of doubt that they take most seriously and unequivocally a pupil-centered approach in their teaching methods. Elliot thus said: Instead of beginning with the beliefs of the churches and thinking of education as a methodology for the transmission of Biblical and doctrinal teachings, they (the leaders in modern religious education) have centered their attention upon the children, young people, and adults who were to be educated.[22] Citing educators from Rousseau down to Pestalozzi, who developed the viewpoint of regarding education as being based on the nature of the child and the natural laws for his growth and who believed that education therefore was basically a "drawing out instead of a pouring in," Elliot adopted the latter's view that "teaching must proceed from the concrete to the abstract," and that "environment or experience of the child is the most valuable means and materials" for instruction. "Observation and investigation instead of memorizing and class discussion, and thinking instead of reciting" characterized Pestalozzi's work, so observed Elliot. Likewise, the basic ideas of Friedrich Froebel, who founded the kindergarten and contributed indirectly to the development of the movement in the United States, include "self-activity determined by the child's interests and desires and intelligently directed,"[23] as essential to the unfolding of the child's inborn capacities.

This pupil-centered methodology also transforms the conception of punishment in an educational process. Again, it must be restated that liberals are not advocates of an attitude in education of 'letting children alone'; proper guidance, and even proper punishment, is administered whenever the occasion warrants it. Whereas the emphasis heretofore was on the personal will and judgment of parents or teachers in the act of punishment as a consequence of certain conduct, it is shifted now for adult and child to look together at the consequences of the action. Such theory and practice of punishment is educative because out of

---

[22] *Ibid.*, p. 3. Also Fahs, *op. cit.*, pp. 196ff.

[23] *Ibid.*, pp. 40f. Compare with Fahs' book, p. 187 where she states that children must "learn through tangible to intangible, concrete to abstract, seen to unseen."

77

it children learn that conduct has consequences which they cannot avoid, life being what it is, and they learn also something of what is right and what is wrong in the true method of judging action by its effects.

These approaches are based on the assumption that human beings have the capacity for choice and that growth takes place through making choices, through acting upon these decisions, and through evaluating the consequences of action. "If children are to grow to maturity in the Christian life, they must increasingly develop in the ability and the willingness to take responsibility for their decisions and for their conduct."[24]

Coe implemented this viewpoint by insisting that "the teacher adjusts himself to the pupil, varying the form of words, the emphasis and angle of thought, and the type of attitude, to suit the age, the experience, and the individuality of the other." "Here, for the first time," he wrote elsewhere, "educational theory provides for real integration of the personality. I, the teacher, cannot integrate the impulses, the values, the choices of a pupil; he must do it himself, or it never will be done."[25]

Pointing his finger to the fact that this pupil-centered theory and practice was gaining acceptance even among conservative forces and evangelical denominations, Coe ventured to prophesy near the end of the book, *What Is Christian Education?*, in the statement quoted below:

> Thorough training, to begin with, will surely move in the general direction of the self-activity principle. You may use as a shibboleth, "pupil-centered," "life-situation," "problem," "project," "freedom," "creativity," or whatever you prefer; you will not go far into the subject before you find yourself committed to the thing toward which these words point. Thus, the study of technic is more than a study of mere technic; it is a study of personality and the laws of its growth, and it develops the kind of respect for the personality of pupils that tends to enfranchize them from all external authority.[26]

2. Experience—or Life-situation—Centered Approach

The other side of the coin in adopting the pupil-centered approach is the experience-centered or life-situation-centered approach. Nothing

---

[24] *Ibid.*, p. 314.

[25] Coe, *What Is Christian Education?*, pp. 25 and 185, respectively.

[26] *Ibid.*, p. 236. Compare with *A Social Theory of Christian Education*, p. 339 where he stated that "liberalism is most concerned that the pupil should weigh facts, and do some real thinking of his own, even if his thoughts do not reproduce those of his teacher."

78

that is a part of the pupils life experience is neglected. Writing on "It Matters How We Gain Our Beliefs," Fahs states that religion is regarded by her as a vital and healthy result of one's own creative thought and feeling and experience as he responds to life in all its fullness.[27] Influences from without and from the past affect the formation of such a religion; but the life-giving element is within the child and in his present experiences. The pupil must be encouraged to think things out for himself and to begin with learning how to live a good life as a matter for experimentation and discovery.[28]

It was Coe's position that it is a perfectly safe assumption that men first attributed ethical love to the divine being after, not before, they had experienced it among themselves. Any learning process begins with here and now; human interactions begin with one another. Here is where one experiences the so-called "indwelling Christ" and the "Holy Spirit" who bears witness to Jesus and to God. He went on to say that "the correct policy for Christian education is now indicated; the learner is to be led, through his acquaintance with the 'witnessing church' to realize the presence and the character of God."[29]

After analyzing some current movements and conditions in education in general and Christian education in particular, Coe had this to say:

> In the churches, as in public-school quarters, awakened thought concerning the process of teaching has circled about three main ideas—interest, activity, and social participation, all on the part of the pupil—with a fourth idea, character, over-arching all three of them like a cloud . . . It is the learner's present purposeful activity, the plans that he makes and executes, his own projects—so the theory goes—that most promotes growth. This, in brief, is the project-principle, which is commonly called project-method . . . A pupil's project may require hand-work; it will require busyness at times, reflection at other times; it may get its start from textbook or teacher, and it may include the systematic study of a definite area of human knowledge, but these enter into a true project, not by imitation, mere suggestion, or authority; they are rather ways of working out free purposes, and they are significant and educative for this reason.[30]

---

[27] Fahs, *op. cit.*, p. 16.

[28] *Ibid.*, p. 29.

[29] Coe, *What Is Christian Education?*, pp. 77f.

[30] *Ibid.*, pp. 183-185. Referral is made to Coe's further statements on this point on pages 226, 239, 249, 284f, and 289. Also in *A Social Theory of Christian Education*, pp. 80, 193f, and 273 where he expounded on so-called "laboratory method."

On December 8, 1922 at the International Council of Religious Education, a committee of eight members was appointed, with Professor William C. Bower as chairman, to undertake the construction of a new International Curriculum. Elliot wrote that the Bower Committee's report recommended a thoroughgoing change in the orientation of religious education. In traditional religious education, the Bible and the accepted doctrinal interpretations are the organizing center and religious education is conceived as an improved methodology for teaching the Bible and Christian truths; in the Bower report life situations are the organizing center and the Bible is utilized as an aid in meeting these situations on a Christian basis. In traditional Protestant religious education, Christian faith and practice are considered as already known, and education is a method of securing their acceptance and application; in the Bower report, what is Christian in faith and practice is to be discovered in and through the educational process. In traditional Protestant religious education, the teaching is a preparation for the experience of conversion; in the Bower report, it is assumed that Christian faith and experience are to be realized through growth from early childhood to adult years.[31]

To Elliot, both Tillich, with terminology which is strange to the average American religious educator, and Coe, in language with which the religious educator is more familiar, "say that God becomes apprehended and experienced only in the concrete situations of life where he is realized in the crucial act of decision."[32] Both scholars, though engaged in different fields of specialization, seem to agree that this direct experience and apprehension of God is defeated where attention is shifted to a God so beyond and unrelated to the human scene that relationship to him is irrelevant to mundane affairs or where through authoritative creed or church he is used as the rationalization of some present belief so that decision is unnecessary.

Experience-centered religious education is far more than a revised and improved teaching method for making a certain religious interpretation understood so that it may be appropriated by individuals and groups, according to Elliot. To those who have such an educational approach, it represents their conviction as to the process through which the Christian religion has developed and through which Christian experience has been realized. "Learning in and through experience,"

---

[31] Elliot, *op. cit.*, pp. 56-62. More discussion was made on life-situation-centered approach on pp. 251-258.

[32] *Ibid.*, p. 275.

Elliot declared, "is not a pedagogical slogan, invented by progressive educators. It is rather a statement of the way mankind has found out everything which is known and has made whatever progress has been attained." He continued:

> Religion is no exception to this dependence upon learning through experience. Everything that man knows about God has grown out of his experience in the world and out of his reflections upon the manifestations of God in nature and in human life . . . Children and young people come to the knowledge of God in the same way that the race has come to its understanding, viz., by their experience with the manifestations of God in human life. Parents and teachers can help in the interpretation of that experience. They can increase its range by providing for youth significant experiences in the present or out of the past. But it is only the manifestations of God which enter the experience that are significant for the individual.[33]

The organization of religious education around the life situations of children, young people, and adults is therefore more than a pedagogical device for motivating subject matter. It is basic to the practice of religious education. Since it is by now accepted that learning takes place in and through experience, a significant educational process must be related to these situations where learning is taking place. Quoting from Nevin Harner in his book, *The Educational Work of the Church*, Elliot made it known that Christian education is an attempt "to discover the divinely ordained process by which individuals grow in Christlikeness, and to work with that process."[34]

3. The Adult as the Helper

In this life-situation and pupil-centered pedagogical approach, the teachers, parents, or elders are constantly standing by to guide, assist, and to provide most favorable conditions, circumstances, and atmospheres in which both pupils and teachers grow together toward Christian understanding and maturity.

Coe depicted a necessary self-appraisal of teachers in Christian education with the following self-directed questions: Am I helping my pupils grow in the personal or ethical-love way of dealing both with themselves and with others whose lives they touch? Am I helping them

---

[33] Read *Ibid.*, pp. 310-313.
[34] Nevin C. Harner, *The Educational Work of the Church*, p. 20; also Elliot, *op. cit.*, p. 313.

extend this fellowship to others who need it? Am I helping them master the conditions of efficient good-will by using the methods of science with reference to all facts involved, whether facts of history, of external nature, or of the mind of man? Am I helping them to such a deep and satisfying experience of this ethical-love way that they are learning to worship?[35]

In trying to help pupils, a teacher must, through the entire execution of a certain project or premeditated experience, always stand by, ready to interject the kind of help that will make the experience of the pupils most educative and creative. Moreover, when using a project-method, the true teacher sees to it that projects progress from level to level; they must be hard enough and illuminating enough to carry pupils beyond what they now are. The project-principles, or experience- and pupil-centered method, evidently does not mean "hands off" on the teacher's part. Quite the contrary; it calls for guidance that is more persuasive than any that the old type of educational method even attempted.[36]

In view of the fact that good teaching must be "pupil-centered" rather than "material-centered," can it be said that whereas the good teacher of yesterday studied content much and the pupil little the teacher of liberal persuasion studies the pupil much and the content little? The answer is, by all means, a resounding "No!". This is not the meaning of the term, "pupil-centered" pedagogy. For the liberal education requires better command of material than ever.

What the teacher is supposed to do amounts to inserting into the "life-situation" something that seems likely to improve it through the pupil's own acts. Coe wrote that:

> The teacher, acting as an experienced friend, may point out something already there in the situation that the pupil had not noticed; show how others in similar situations have acted, and what the results were; or strengthen one desire as against another by holding attention to it or by subjecting it to some social judgment. Material or content (by which is meant ideas already in the minds of the elders) is now thought of, not as something to be "gotten over" at all costs, but as a source of possible help, to be used or not as occasion seems to require.[37]

[35] Coe, What Is Christian Education?, p. 178.

[36] Ibid., p. 187. On page 66 in A Social Theory of Christian Education is found Coe's "Theory of Gradation."

[37] Ibid., p. 191.

Elsewhere,[38] Coe supported this argument by defining the function of instruction as to assist the child to analyze the situations, purposes, and activities with which he has to do, so that impulsive goodness shall grow into a deliberate good will; so that the sphere of the good will shall be better and better understood; so that co-operation in social causes shall be organized on a wider and wider scale and with ever-increasing efficiency, and so that all the resources of a cultivated spirit may be known and made available for all.

4. Reason in Studies

In order that the pupil may study critically and intelligently of the past and present, and of all fields of learning opened to him, he must be taught first of all to employ fully his rational capacity and also to extend it. Coe said that religious education must include "measures for inducing pupils to employ their capacity for knowing, and for organizing life by means of thought." Picking out the Roman Catholic teaching as the best example, he criticized the main tradition of religious education, Christian as well as non-Christian, as far as knowledge and thinking are concerned. He stated that the religious educational enterprises utilize the exercise of the intelligence to a very limited degree and then stops—often not only stopping but blocking the way to further use.[39]

Defending more forcefully and in greater detail the importance of the place reason or intelligence occupies in the liberal approach, Coe stated:

> This is not a narrower or less intellectual conception of Christian instruction than the one that takes its starting-point from the dogmatic-intellectualistic notion of divine revelation. Stimulus for intellectual activity is here, and the interest to which appeal is made is as broad as the Christian ideal itself. Anything in history, literature or doctrine that actually illuminates the path of active love, any kind of knowledge that can be turned into power for social living, anything that imagination or discursive reason can contribute to thoroughly socialized satisfactions—all this belongs within Christian instruction under the social presuppositions that we have adopted.[40]

---

[38] Coe, A Social Theory of Christian Education, p. 82.
[39] See Coe, What Is Christian Education?, pp. 129f.
[40] Coe, A Social Theory of Christian Education, p. 82.

And again:

> The mental operation that is chiefly required for religious growth is the discriminative appreciation of value. This involves, of course, observation of facts, some understanding of the past, and some rational foresight; it involves some generalization of the standpoint from which one judges life and duty; but here the main work of intelligence is to clarify one's desires and purposes so that revision may be made, and to discover means whereby one's life purposes may be carried out. The achievement of a broad outlook, then, or of ability to prove or defend one's position by sound knowledge is at most a single part, and that not the central part, of religious instruction.[41]

From the above quotations, it is unmistakably clear that part of the inherent ingredient in the pedagogical principle explicitly adhered to by liberal religious educators is their willingness and openness toward any honest inquiry into not only the present but also the past and future as well. They also open themselves to any insights, wisdom, or contributions made, or potentially to be made, from all disciplines of learning. Even a liberal among liberals, such as Fahs, admits that "there are treasures in old dust of ages" in what she calls the "old Story of Salvation."[42] The uncovering of treasures in old dust of ages is not confined to the studies of the Bible, however. She maintains that study of other religions and "Bibles" is both necessary and profitable. The universal note should be heard even at the very beginning of a child-education and it needs continuous emphasis during the pre-adolescent years, as well as the rest of his life.[43]

Returning to Coe, the principles of scientific method, to him, are not only valid, they are a necessity for spiritual health; they are a part of pure and undefiled religion. To summarize what he elaborated as the principles of scientific method, one finds the six categories listed below.

(1) Intellectual co-operation.

(2) No foreigners, no social classes, no special privileges, no intellectual or hierarchical prerogatives.

(3) Eagerness to learn, not to teach, in the sense of inducing another to conform to what already is in one's mind.

(4) Though the sciences employ every type of logical procedure, they are particularly reliant upon observed fact as compared with reliance upon the self-consistency of a thought structure.

---

[41] *Ibid.*, pp. 339f.

[42] Fahs, *op. cit.*, pp. 94f.

[43] *Ibid.*, p. 97. Also p. 197.

(5) By the use of hypothesis, experiment, and mathematical analysis for the purpose of extending the range and the fineness of direct observation, and for supplementing it.

(6) There is no obligatory proposition, no orthodoxy.[44]

IV. THE PEDAGOGICAL PRINCIPLES OF RECONSTRUCTED LIBERAL CHRISTIAN EDUCATORS

A. IMPLICIT STATEMENTS ON PEDAGOGICAL PRINCIPLES

1. What Is a Method?

Through the study of their writings, it is discovered that both Miller and Wyckoff emphasized strongly the point of relevance in their teachings on method in Christian education. Method, in Miller's opinion, "is the way in which the learner is led to see the relevance of subject matter to the problems of his own life."[45] If the learner's problem and concerns are religious—and according to Miller any problem or concern may be religious—method is the means whereby the resources of a religious tradition are made relevant to that problem in everyday experience. Miller goes on to state that the purpose of method is to make a student think, and thinking is facing a real problem with the total resources of one's person, involving, therefore, the resources of the community and whatever comes through these channels from God. The subject matter may come from knowledge of the past, of current ways of solving problems, of lesson materials and resources, and of one's own way of achieving results.

Expressing it in a somewhat different way, Miller wrote in 1961 in *Christian Nurture and the Church* that method is simply the means whereby relevant theological truths are connected with the interests, problems, and meanings in the lives of the learners.[46] This naturally is always something dynamic, involving a two-way communication based on the significance of the persons and the revelation of God seen as at work in the process of education.

Wyckoff shows his understanding and definition of method in Christian teaching by answering his own question, "What is a method?":

It is a form of systematic procedure for accomplishing an educational task. It is an activity used in learning. Thus a Christian

---

[44] Coe, *A Social Theory of Christian Education*, pp. 137-139.

[45] Randolph C. Miller, *Education for Christian Living*, p. 159.

[46] Miller, *Christian Nurture and the Church*, p. 186.

education method is a means or plan for getting some aspect of the Christian education job done . . . The heart of method is to engage in the life the church lives and the work it does. It is the living of the Christian life, under experienced guidance, as it is most appropriately lived at each stage of the individual development.[47]

He contends that effective method in Christian education will open God's word to the learner and teach him to read, to listen, to hear, and to decide what the word means to him, and then to live accordingly. Effective method thus described depends upon doing these things and associating closely with those who can give out of the fullness of their own experience the kind of direction that will keep the learner from making harmful mistakes or getting off the track.

2. Clues in Christian Education Method

As a scholar in whose book, *The Dynamics of Christian Education*, the concept of kerygma is central, Cully upholds that the very proclamation of the good news is teaching. The proclamation is this: The new age has dawned. Jesus the Christ, who was sent by God, has brought it through his living and dying and his resurrection. He is the living Lord who through the work of the Holy Spirit is recreating lives through his power in the church. Turn around; accept the gift offered by God which is his forgiveness; receive the Holy Spirit; and become partakers of eternal life now and evermore.

This is not "teaching" in the sense of the imparting of information. It is "the dynamic word through which a redemptive experience is mediated. The way in which it is proclaimed as well as the fact of its proclamation gives a ground for interpreting the experience."[48] She means to say that when the impact of kerygma is felt and the person is turned around—accepting the forgiveness of God, finding new life in Jesus Christ, and opening himself for further instruction and enlightenment through Christian fellowship—then the person has a proper ground for interpreting and imparting the experience.

In order that one may rightly proclaim, he must first of all study the Bible and theology with utmost sincerity and diligence in faith. To Cully, a new methodology—which she terms an existential method—is indicated when the Bible is taken seriously as the Word of God to man.

---

[47] D. Campbell Wyckoff, *The Gospel and Christian Education*, p. 147.
[48] Iris V. Cully, *The Dynamics of Christian Education*, p. 48. See also pp. 56f.

To Miller, as expressed in *The Clue to Christian Education*, there are two reasons behind his searchng for a new clue to Christian education: his detection of (1) increasing dissatisfaction with the content-centered teaching method which is still prevalent, and (2) widespread distrust of the so-called life-centered-only teaching. He observes that the modern philosophy of educational method has been "sound at the expense of theology, while both true and false theologies have been presented without the methods to bring them to life in the experiences of the learners."[49] He acknowledges, however, that experience- or project-centered method is worthwhile and exciting enough to keep the pupil occupied, and as far as methodology is concerned it is fundamentally sound, but—and this is unquestionably an all-important 'but'— unless something new is added unto it, it will result in an actual stoppage of Christian growth. The examples on the other side, meaning ungraded material, catechism teaching method, are equally futile and frustrating. Miller maintains that "The one missing topic in most educational schemes today is theology, and in theology properly interpreted lies the answer to most of the pressing educational problems of the day."[50]

3. Content Plus Experience

Miller specifies that one new element in the educational theory of this generation is the discovery of the organic relation between doctrine and experience, between content and method, and between truth and life.[51] The center of Christian education curriculum is a two-fold relationship between God and the learner. The curriculum should be both God-centered and experience-centered. In order to place God and man at the center of the Christian educational method, Christian educators must have adequate knowledge of the nature and working of both God and man and of God's relationships to particular pupils.

---

[49] Miller, *The Clue to Christian Education*, p. 2.

[50] *Ibid.*, p. 4.

Note: This quotation was also used by Dr. Norma H. Thompson of New York University in her doctoral dissertation, page 46. On the same page, she again quoted from Miller's same book, page 15, where he made a concise statement about what he means by the word, 'clue': The clue is the rediscovery of a relevant theology which will bridge the gap between content and method, providing the background and perspective of Christian truth by which the best methods and content will be used as tools to bring the learners into the right relationship with the living God who is revealed to us in Jesus Christ, using the guidance of parents and the fellowship of life in the church as the environment in which Christian nurture will take place.

[51] *Ibid.*

According to Miller, the battleground of religious living, including Christian teaching and learning, is the area of faith rather than belief, of experience rather than dogma, of grace and forgiveness rather than creeds. "But the theologizing which (William) James says is 'after effects' is equally important, for we need to know what faith is in order to guide our ways of living."[52]

Wyckoff also advocates a content plus experience centered approach to this question. He observes that of late years there has been a great deal of discussion of the relative merits of transmissive and creative methods in Christian education. He answers succinctly that the choice between them is an unnecessary one. Christian educators can know clearly what is to be transmitted or communicated to the child, the youth, and the adult. Usually the method that will be used will be one in which the individual and the group recreate the experience.

Wyckoff presumes that all Christians accept the point that the teachers or parents are not satisfied unless the Christian faith is really learned and grasped by the pupils. They all feel that there are definite propositions, definite content, and definite subject matter in Christian faith that must be learned. On the other hand, they are also concerned about starting always with pupils' experiences. They are haunted, Wyckoff says, by the feeling that possibly if they use this experience-centered approach too consistently the children or youth will not be introduced to all the necessary aspects of Christian faith.

It is a question that need not plague the educators so seriously as it has, Wyckoff continues. For it is very possible for them to use the experience of the pupil and at the same time be assured that they shall not miss the riches and the fullness of Christian truth and faith. He prescribes that in order to effect this combination of subject matter and experience in one unified concept of education, there are three principles that are needed:

(1) Experience for any human being is continuous.
(2) The development of personality takes place through experience.
(3) The above two principles bring into focus the matter of subject matter or content. It is the principle of the guidance and enrichment of experience.[53]

---

[52] *Ibid.*, p. 105.
[53] Read Wyckoff, *The Task of Christian Education*, pp. 51-53.

As will be pointed out later,[54] Cully stresses most emphatically the essentiality of life-situation in a teaching method. However, she does not emphasize the life-situation aspect of teaching method to the extent of neglecting or forgetting the content in a teaching process. She claims that her "emphasis on the kerygma is not intended to be made at the expense of an interpretation of the didache" because didache includes an understanding of the beliefs of the church, the teaching that arises from the kerygma itself. She urges that stories, conversations, and discussions should be concerned with the content of faith, such as the doctrine of God, Christology, the doctrines of the Holy Spirit, salvation, and eschatology.[55]

Sherrill implements the other three authors by stating that the Christian truth can be communicated and imparted only within the context of Christian love. This love, which is agape in Greek, can be communicated to even the very young in the fellowship of Christian family and church. This means, Sherrill presses on, that the essence of revelation which the Bible records can begin to reach the very young before they can understand one word of speech. As Tillich has shown, Sherrill rightly observed, that this love, agape, is itself creative and is the true ground of Christian education.[56] This is what Sherrill means by what he calls "The principle of nonverbal communication." This is what he has to say:

> Since the earliest communication in which the self participates is nonverbal, and since at all ages nonverbal communication is a channel for two-way communication of feeling and emotion, this form of communication must be taken into account in using Biblical materials as well as all other materials . . . When it comes to the formal use of Biblical materials, the nonverbal undertones and overtones which accompany the use of the material in teaching are powerful factors in the interaction between selves."[57]

4. Insights of Other Disciplines Utilized

Wyckoff's personal inclination in respect to the pedagogical principles is shown through his adoption of the definition of religious edu-

---

[54] See pages 182-184.
[55] Cully, op. cit., p. 163.
[56] Lewis J. Sherrill, The Gift of Power, p. 179. The reference to Tillich is found in "Creative Love in Education," World Christian Education, 1963, pp. 70 and 75.
[57] Ibid., pp. 186 f.

cation made by the late Samuel L. Hamilton of the Department of Religious Education, New York University. It reads as follows:

> Religious education is the guided process of helping growing persons to achieve at each stage of their growth such habits, skills, attitudes, appreciations, knowledges, ideas, ideals, and intentions as will enable them at each stage to achieve an ever more integrated personality, competent and satisfying living in their social environment, and increasing co-operativeness with God and man in the reconstruction of society into a fellowship of persons.[58]

To attain this high aim, psychological, sociological, philosophical, and theological understandings that relate to the nature and needs of the pupils must be used. One must not be so negligent as to forget that the utilization of all these tools and disciplines has a definite purpose. They must contribute to the creative process that Christians, young or old, see happening in themselves. Rebirth and re-creation in a Christian cannot take place—at least rebirth and re-creation that involve intelligent espousal of the Christian faith—without a background of the knowledge of what the Christian faith means. But this rebirth process, dependent as it usually is upon the transmission of the Christian faith and Christian doctrine, is primarily a matter of the re-creation of human experience into experience that is divinely redeemed. Methods in Christian education, at home or in the church, are processes, therefore, which are dynamic in character, through which the personal, the social, and the divine elements integrate to promote growth in Christian character and living.[59]

Elaborating on the use of different disciplines several years later in another book,[60] Wyckoff states that various disciplines, such as systematic theology, philosophy, philosophy of education, history, history of education, psychology, educational psychology, sociology, educational sociology, and communications are the foundations from which the two major concerns of Christian education theory, namely, theology and science of education, stem. In a way, they sum up the disciplines in terms of their most significant present impact on the field of Christian education. His own position on this point is that Christian education can and must be theologically thorough and accurate and at the same time maintain educational integrity and soundness. In a classroom teach-

---

[58] Wyckoff, *The Task of Christian Education*, p. 18.
[59] *Ibid.*, p. 139.
[60] Wyckoff, *The Gospel and Christian Education*, pp. 75f.

ing situation, subject matter in theology, Bible, or other fields is employed at every point but it is always employed in the context of changing and developing learning experiences.

Seconding Wyckoff's argument, Miller urges that the reconstructed liberals should use all the insights of modern science and theory in education, but the assumptions of the "secularists" about the nature of the world and of man are not the Christian's assumptions, he warns. This is the way he puts it:

> We begin with the truth that is ours as Christians, and because all facts and observations are assumed to be consistent with the one area of truth and revelation which comes from God, we may then use the observations, experiments, and insights of non-Christian truth . . . The educational philosophy of John Dewey, for example, is of supreme importance to anyone dealing with educational process, yet his theory of truth is almost negative. A theological critique of his goals and methods enables us to make full use of the valuable contributions of America's most influential educator without sacrificing our Christian perspectives and goals.[61]

Touching specifically on methods, Miller avers that "we desire methods of learning that are consistent with the insights of theology into the nature of man, using the assistance of the discoveries of all the related sciences and arts of education."[62] It is his contention that child psychology, educational psychology, the sociology of learning, the psychology of religion, and psychiatry all have contributions to make to the teaching methods in Christian education. What is needed is an educational philosophy that is sound, adequate, and relevant from the standpoint of theology, psychology, pedagogy, sociology, and history, with a realistic appraisal of resources for fulfilling these goals in today's world.

B. EXPLICIT STATEMENTS ON TEACHING METHODS

1. Life-centered Approach

Cully makes it clear beyond any question that she favors a life-centered method in Christian teaching. This is amply proved by the frequency with which she openly advocates and discusses this approach.[63]

---

[61] Miller, *Education for Christian Living*, pp. 7f.
[62] *Ibid.*, p. 18.
[63] Cully, *op. cit.*, pp. 119, 129f, 143, 155f, etc.

She says that methods for Christian teaching should be life-centered, and adds that life-centered method usually means experience-centered method.[64]

The central element in a life-centered approach, for Cully, is the concept of participation. It means an existential involvement on the pupil's as well as the teacher's part. She states explicitly: "Participation is a central factor in life-centered teaching."[65] Focusing her attention on the point of the pupil's participation, she writes that in order that the pupil will truly learn he should have the opportunity to fully participate through his present experience. The task of Christian nurture is to put his present experience in a context that will give him something to remember. "He will remember that which has relevance," she continues, "and will participate in those events and persons in the past history of the church which will help and sustain him."[66]

Even after switching over to the subject of the teacher in her discourse, she sustains her stress on the idea of participation. To her, the pupil participates through the teacher, which means that the teacher himself is a median for the pupil's participation. "The teacher is a guide as well as a fellow participant with the child,"[67] she says.

She goes on to state that life-centered methods include ways for participation in those historic events in the Bible and the church through which God's saving activity is known. They include ways by which the child, through such participation, comes into a recognition that God speaks to him here and now and seeks to give him integration of the self through the Holy Spirit in the life of the church.[68] Even the groups that traditionally have used more coercive and imposition methods through catechism and the creed are rethinking their methods, in order to make them vivid and dynamic by relating their meanings to the life of the child before he comes to an age for memorizing the words.

Sherrill, like Coe among liberals, readily acknowledges his indebtedness to and high estimate of John Dewey's work. As far as changes in persons are concerned, Dewey's theory has signal value in at least two respects, Sherrill admits. One is the importance attached to the individual's own experience in the learning process. The other is the

---

[64] *Ibid.*, p. 119.
[65] *Ibid.*
[66] *Ibid.*, p. 130.
[67] *Ibid.*, p. 133.
[68] *Ibid.*, p. 156.

importance attached to the sharing of experience, so that learning becomes a social experience.[69]

Writing on the use of the Biblical materials in teaching-learning process in Christian education, Sherrill states that if it is accepted that the chief purpose in using the Bible in the Christian community is that of preparing the way for the continuing encounter with God, methods should be sought which will help people of today to stand inside the Biblical personalities and events and to participate with them in their encounter with God centuries ago. In any such use of the Bible, the Bible becomes part of the living environment that surrounds the learners as well as the teacher in the Christian community. This is what Sherrill calls "The principle of participation." Furthermore, when one is afforded the opportunity for genuine participation in the Bible, he can expect to find some degree of identification taking place. If the learners and the teacher stand beside the Biblical personalities and participate with them, they are no longer mere objects to be objectively studied. By participating, the participants themselves become existentially involved. This is what Sherrill terms "The principle of identification."[70]

2. The Principles of Grading and Readiness

As was pointed out on page 88, Wyckoff regards experience as most important in the teaching of Christian faith through the impartation of the Biblical, theological, and historical content. He then in the next breath brings out the subsequent point in this experience-centered approach; that is, the materials must be graded to fit the pupil's need, capacity, and readiness. He says that it is essential to recognize that the content and subject matter of the Christian faith must at every point be graded: graded to pupil need, graded to pupil capacity, graded to pupil interest—in a word, graded to the readiness of the pupil to respond. This is why it is so crucial for the teacher to know intimately well every child in his class or every young person in his group. This is how he says it:

> If we do not know our children and young people as individuals, how can we go about the process of grading subject matter and experience to their need, capacity, and interest? If the teacher gives them a chance to be known, they will make themselves known,

---

[69] Sherrill, op. cit., p. 152.
[70] Ibid., p. 187.

and the teacher will have some clue as to how to grade the material to the point where there is active need, real capacity, and urgent interest.[71]

For example, it is taken for granted that any teacher will wholeheartedly support the argument that the stories and ideas in the Bible are to be taught in accordance with the capacity of the learner to grasp and understand them. This is what Wyckoff designates "The principle of grading." Then, the stories and ideas of the Bible are to be taught in accordance with the learner's need for them and his interest in learning them. This is "The principle of readiness."[72]

3. The Principle of Variety in Methods

The principles of grading and readiness brings up automatically the next principle. It is the principle of variety in methods. A pupil can be taught through the processes of guided study, of fellowship, involving recreation, of social action, and of worship.[73] Wyckoff interprets that God himself employs various methods in his teaching: demonstrating, telling, and reminding man of his nature, existence, and truth.[74] It is Wyckoff's assumption that constant repetition of a single method does not accomplish the task of building Christian personality and Christian community effectively as a rule.

He concludes that the various types of work the church carries on, such as study, creative expression, action, stewardship, fellowship, worship, etc., involve methods in Christian education. In fact, they are the prime methods of Christian education.[75] These are the means that are intrinsic to the church and thus are the heart of its educational procedures. They are the ways in which Christian education may proceed with nurture in the light of the gospel.

---

[71] Wyckoff, *The Task of Christian Education*, pp. 55f.

[72] *Ibid.*, p. 70.

[73] *Ibid.*, pp. 31f.
Note: On pages 80-82 of the same book, Wyckoff writes that tools that can be employed in man's search after God's truth, beauty, and goodness are: 1. experience. 2. reason. 3. intuition. and 4. revelation.

[74] *Ibid.*, p. 68.

[75] Wyckoff, *The Gospel and Christian Education*, pp. 148f. On pages 131-132, he says, "Christian education's task is the nurture of the Christian life. This is done, in actual fact, in many places, under many circumstances, sometimes in planned ways, and sometimes in unplanned ways . . . Flexibility means guaranteeing adaptability in terms of the educational settings where the curriculum is to be used, in terms of method, and in terms of individual, community, and cultural differences."

Writing on the topic of the "Types and Selection of Method," Miller touches on (1) the material-centered method, (2) Bible-centered method, (3) church-centered method, and (4) doctrine-centered method.[76] He states that once the session is under way, the subject matter generally determines the method. The procedure now is to arrange the resources so that they are effective in the lives of the pupils. Normally, he continues, a combination of methods is desirable in the course of the class session—showing, telling, exchanging ideas, group planning and activity. Cully implements this principle of variety in methods by accepting various arts as media for participation. They are: painting, pictures, music, drama, poetry, story, and writing among others. Extra learning experiences should derive from the experience of an I-thou encounter, decision-making, conversation and discussion, questions, insight, prayer, worship, and witness.[77]

Sherrill is most frank in his admission of personal preference in seeing the combination of methods at work in Christian instruction. He states bluntly that no one method should have an exclusive monopoly over the others. "The history of Christian education," he informs the readers, "is full of instances of idolatrous respect for any method one may mention." Hence one is put on guard against adopting some particular method as the method for Christian education. Equally, one is put on guard against "fleeing from one fad to another in educational method in search of an educational city of refuge where he can dwell in safety with no haunting fear of failure to pursue him."[78] A logical deduction may be made from this that any one particular method possesses the potential of turning into the demonic: such as the time when it lacks or loses spirituality; or if persons involved lose sight of the reality and meaning of interaction taking place; or the relation of material to the pupils is totally severed. On the other hand, any method has the potentiality of being, and possibility of becoming, a spiritual instrument. Great and wise teachers have always used a range of methods so wide and diverse as to be quite embarrassing to the educational theorists and perplexing to the amateurs.

---

[76] Miller, *Education for Christian Living*, pp. 173-175.
[77] Cully, *op. cit.*, pp. 136-150.
[78] Sherrill, *op. cit.*, p. 185.

CHAPTER VII

Summary and Conclusion

There are three separate and distinct parts which constitute this final chapter of the thesis. The first part is a summary of the unique characteristics of the pedagogical principles of each of the three groups in Christian education as revealed through their respective spokesmen and set forth in the preceding two chapters, namely, Chapters V and VI. The second part is composed of a list of characteristics mutually shared by (1) The conservative and liberal groups, (2) The conservative and reconstructed liberal groups, (3) The liberal and reconstructed liberal groups, and (4) All three groups. The third part is comprised of findings and conclusions in which, among others, the two hypotheses set forth on page 5 of this thesis will either be sustained or nullified. The first hypothesis is: the concept of theonomy in Tillich's thought is intimately related to some of the most important ideas in his theology —such ideas as autonomy and heteronomy. This will be proved by the study of the content presented in Chapters III and IV. The second hypothesis is: Tillich's concept of theonomy is most compatible with the pedagogical principles of the reconstructed liberal group in Christian education, his concept of heteronomy with the pedagogical principles of the conservative group, and his concept of autonomy with those of the liberal group. A comparison of the three concepts of theonomy, autonomy, and heteronomy in Tillich's thought with the pedagogical principles in three distinct groups in the Protestant Christian education will be undertaken in the hope of either sustaining or nullifying this hypothesis.

I.   THE CHARACTERISTICS OF THE PEDAGOGICAL
PRINCIPLES OF THREE GROUPS IN
CHRISTIAN EDUCATION

The summarized statements below are either indicative of or clearly show the unique characteristics of the pedagogical principles adhered

to, both implicitly and explicitly, by respective spokesmen in three theologically distinctive groups in Christian education.

A. THE CHARACTERISTICS OF THE PEDAGOGICAL PRINCIPLES OF THE CONSERVATIVE GROUP

1. A real task in Christian teaching method is to discover God's
ways by the work of the Holy Spirit and to work with him.

2. The gateway to the discovery of God's ways of teaching is to believe in and commit oneself wholly to God, Jesus Christ, and the
truths contained in the Holy Scriptures. Faith over reason, divine enlightenment over human search is the key of this point.

3. The center and foundation of a conservative theology as well as
conservative Christian education is bi-polar: it is rooted squarely on
the sovereignty of Christ, the Son of God, and the inerrant authority
of the Holy Scriptures, the written Word of God.

4. Authoritarian, transmissive, or rote method in teaching is unambiguously rejected.

5. All insights gained in fields other than Christian education are
accepted and utilized after careful scrutiny. All means, aspects, and
fields of learning, religious or secular, are regarded as channels to God's
truth.

6. Methodology in conservative Christian education is very deci-
sively experience- and pupil-centered. Or, in other words, the real life-
situation approach is the core of its pedagogy.

7. Curriculum must be graded according to the pupil's level of mental development and abilities.

8. The use of human reason is not rejected. Rather, the conservatives
try to cultivate what one may call a consecrated intellect or a divinely
inspired reason in their teaching-and-learning process.

9. Content plus experience, or outer and inner factors, are equally
emphasized. The balance and equilibrium of both elements in education is the goal.

10. Creative Christian teaching involves (a) prayerful preparation,
(b) willingness to let the Holy Spirit guide and shift, (c) readiness
to follow the lead of the pupils, and (d) various methods are used to
make the outer content an inner experience.

B. The Characteristics of the Pedagogical Principles of the Liberal Group

1. The scientific, objective, and anthropocentric approach is most manifest in the liberals' teaching methods.

2. Teaching methods are regarded not as static tools but as living and moving parts of collective life that have always to be improved.

3. The instruction is to increase the pupil's knowledge, open the world of religious appreciation, induce self-discipline, enlarge his purposes, and develop his judgment and initiative. Thus understood, teaching technique is as spiritual as any Biblical or religious content can possibly be.

4. Authoritarian, transmissive, and imposition theory is outrightly rejected.

5. Freedom, particularly on and from the pupil's part, is most strongly emphasized and maintained in the liberals' pedagogical principle.

6. It is pupil-centered.

7. It is also definitely experience and life-situation centered.

8. The project method is used by the teacher to guide, assist, and provide for the pupils the most favorable conditions, circumstances, and atmospheres in which both pupils and teacher grow together toward Christian understanding and maturity.

9. Adherence to openness toward any honest scientific enquiry into the present, future, and the past is one of the marks in the liberals' teaching method. This principle extends to the disciplines of learning other than that of the religious field and a full utilization of the discoveries and conclusions therefrom.

10. The social aspect of religious enterprises is strongly upheld and proclaimed by the representatives of the liberal camp.

C. The Characteristics of the Pedagogical Principles of the Reconstructed Liberal Group

1. Relevance—relevance particularly of content to method—occupies the core of major concern in the pedagogical principles of Christian education among the reconstructed liberals.

2. The very proclamation of the good news as discovered in the Holy Scriptures, presented systematically in theology, and its impact

experienced existentially by the listeners is in itself a form of Christian teaching and they—the Bible, theology, and the saving experience—constitute essential clues in Christian education methodology.

3. A content plus experience approach is unanimously advocated.

4. The insights of other disciplines are utilized within the framework of Christian truth for the purpose of contributing to the creative process that the pupils see happening in themselves.

5. Life-centered approach is adhered to by the spokesmen in this group.

6. The lesson materials must be graded according to the pupil's need, capacity, and interest. In other words, the content of Christian education must be graded in the light of the readiness at each stage of the pupil's development.

7. A combination of various methods in teaching process is most desirable in Christian education.

II. THE CHARACTERISTICS MUTUALLY SHARED

A. The Characteristics of the Pedagogical Principles Mutually Shared by the Conservative and Liberal Groups

1. The scientific attitude and rational approach are embraced by both the conservative and liberal groups.

2. The teaching method is not static but responsive and creative.

3. An authoritarian method is definitely rejected.

4. The pupil-centered approach is accepted.

5. A content plus experience or outer plus inner approach is advocated.

6. The application of a variety of methods is a rule rather than an exception.

7. The insights and contributions of fields other than Christian education are accepted and utilized.

B. The Characteristics of the Pedagogical Principles Mutually Shared by the Conservative and Reconstructed Liberal Groups

1. Belief in God and personal commitment to his work through Jesus Christ are essential ingredients in Christian pedagogical principles.

2. Teaching methods in Christian education must be creative and flexible.

3. The pupil's experience is a center around which the whole curriculum in Christian education is constructed and put into practice.

4. Both outer and inner factors are equally emphasized.

5. The use of a variety of methods in teaching is accepted without question.

6. The discoveries, insights, and theories in other disciplines of learning are accepted and applied to a Christian educational teaching-learning process wherever and whenever they are applicable and practiceable.

C. The Characteristics of the Pedagogical Principles Mutually Shared by the Liberal and Reconstructed Liberal Groups

1. The scientific, rational, and systematic approach is one of the common characteristics of these two groups.

2. The Christian teaching methods are not static but flexible.

3. An authoritarian, imposition theory is rejected.

4. The experience- and pupil-centered approach is freely accepted.

5. The content and personal response and experience of pupils are both regarded as essential in a teaching-learning situation.

6. Various methods are used in accordance with the demands of the situation and the levels of the pupils.

7. The insights, methodologies, and philosophies in other branches of learning are accepted and utilized when they do not contradict religious convictions.

D. The Characteristics of the Pedagogical Principles Shared by All Three Groups

1. The teaching methods in Christian education are not static but creative and responsive.

2. An imposition, authoritarian, or rote method is rejected.

3. An experience- and pupil-centered approach is accepted as a necessary and correct one.

4. The desirability of the use of rational powers is upheld.

5. Both outer and inner elements are emphasized.

6. The acceptance of the employment of various methods according,

and in response to, the needs of an educational situation is one of the common characteristics in all three groups.

7. Many insights and possible contributions to be made by other disciplines of learning and walks of life are received and applied to the teaching aspect of Christian education.

III.   FINDINGS AND CONCLUSIONS

A.   The First Hypothesis Is Sustained

From the data presented in Chapters III and IV, it is discovered that the first hypothesis in this thesis is correct and must be sustained: that the concept of theonomy in Tillich's thought is intimately related to some of the most important ideas in his theology—such ideas as autonomy and heteronomy.

It was pointed out in the presentation of the concept of theonomy in Chapter III that Tillich very frequently mentioned and related the concept of either autonomy or heteronomy, or both, in his discourses on the concept of theonomy.[1] Conversely, in his elucidation of the concepts of autonomy and heteronomy Tillich often related them to the concept of theonomy.[2] He stated explicitly that theonomy is the transcendent foundation which gives both autonomy and heteronomy depth, unity, and ultimate meaning. "Theonomy is prior to both; they are elements within it. But theonomy, at the same time, is posterior to both; they tend to be reunited in the theonomy from which they come."[3] Their interrelationship sometimes takes a negative form. Tillich wrote that one of the characteristics of theonomy is "its permanent struggle against both an independent heteronomy and an independent autonomy."[4] This quotation reinforces the finding that, both positively and negatively, theonomy is related to the concepts of autonomy and heteronomy.

More specifically, Tillich states that theonomy does not mean a law of God which is imposed upon man from a supernatural sphere. So interpreted, theonomy would mean nothing but heteronomy. Theonomy

---

[1] See the following pages in this thesis: pp. 16f, 19, 24, 26, 29, 31, and 35.
[2] See pp. 38, 39 (Footnote number 10), 39-44, 47f, and 50-55.
[3] Page 16. See also *ST III*, p. 251.
[4] *Ibid.*

means rather that the forms of autonomy point beyond themselves, without being destroyed or interfered with on their own ground, to the ground from which they come, and which they reflect and form and shape. It affirms the autonomous forms of creative process. Autonomy is always present as a tendency in a theonomous situation; it acts under the surface of every theonomy.

Over and against autonomous independence, heteronomous elements tend to move instinctively in humans in the direction of the repression of and aggression toward autonomous thought. In heteronomy the broken symbols of myth and cult press in from the outside and prevent the mind from developing its autonomous structure.[5] All finite and preliminary concerns possess tyrannical elements in demanding man's ultimate concern and infinite devotion. Likewise, every finite thing—be it work, pleasure, money, science, a person, or nation—in its heteronomous form demands man's whole heart and his whole mind and his whole strength and orders him to transform it into his ultimate concern, that is, his god.[6]

In theonomy, the divine being transforms all the preliminary authorities and concerns into media of himself. They then become in the process and as its natural consequence tools to make God's will shine through and thereby create a theonomous state in an individual, a society, a culture, or an age.

Tillich concluded that both autonomy and heteronomy are rooted in theonomy and that each goes astray when their basic unity is broken. A permanent struggle between autonomous independence and heteronomous reaction, or heteronomous suppression and autonomous reaction, leads to the quest for a new theonomy. Revelation from the transcendental sphere overcomes the conflict between autonomy and heteronomy by reestablishing their essential unity. A perfect theonomy keeps autonomous reason from losing its depth and from becoming empty and open to demonic intrusions and, on the other hand, keeps heteronomous reason from establishing itself against rational autonomy or from destroying the structural laws of autonomous reason from the outside.[7]

The foregoing summary statements show that Tillich's concept of theonomy is indeed inseparably related to the concepts of autonomy and heteronomy in his thought.

---

[5] Page 51.
[6] Page 47.
[7] Page 55.

It is also discovered that the concepts of theonomy, autonomy, and
heteronomy in Tillich's thought are not only intimately interrelated but
also intrinsically interpenetrated with some other major theological
concepts in his system—such concepts as God, the Spiritual Presence,
the New Being, Jesus Christ, church, faith, reason, culture, history,
and kairos.

1. God

According to Tillich himself the idea of God is the foundation of
every theological thought.[8] As the etymology of the term indicates,
theonomy is concerned with nomos, law, and theos, or God. Tillich
spoke of God as the creative ground of everything, who is always present, and always experienced as a being who is nearer to man than he
is to himself. He is the object of man's every ultimate concern.

2. The Spiritual Presence

As God is omnipresent, so is his Spirit and his Kingdom. In fact,
God cannot be known to anyone at any time except through his Spiritual
Presence. And whenever and wherever the divine Spirit is present, there
theonomy will be established.[9] Tillich contended that there is a universal quest for a new theonomy in all corners of the world and this
quest can be answered by the impact of the Spiritual Presence in all
individuals, religious institutions, and cultural forms. Wherever there
is theonomy, traces of the impact of the Spiritual Presence are visible.

3. The New Being in Jesus the Christ

The dynamics of the Spiritual Presence in mankind must be seen
in a threefold sense: first, in mankind as a whole in preparation for the
central manifestation of the divine Spirit; second, in the divine Spirit's
basic manifestation itself; and third, in the emergence of the holy community under the theonomous impact of the central event. Jesus Christ
is the divine Spirit's basic manifestation itself, Tillich said. He is the
New Being in which the self-estrangement of man's existence is overcome. The New Being as embodied in Jesus the Christ is a reality of

---

[8] Page 18.
[9] Page 19.

103

reconciliation and reunion, of creativity, meaning, and hope.[10] His task is to conquer the existential estrangement of the human situation, and to establish a new reality from which the demonic powers or structure of destruction are excluded. Jesus the Christ was the actual embodiment of this New Being in human history because he had a complete and uninterrupted unity with God throughout his earthly life. In other words, he was the one, and the only one, who was able to keep the theonomous state unbroken at all times.

4. The Church

Deriving from this central event in the history of human race under the theonomous impact is the holy community which in its manifest form is called the church. It is a community of people who accept in faith the appearance of the New Being in Jesus Christ as God's gift to them for their salvation. The church is the spiritual community in its receptive stage. The church regards itself as the embodiment of the New Being and the creation of the Spiritual Presence. It is primarily a group of people who express a new reality by which they have been grasped. It is where the New Being is really real and where one can make the New Being an actuality. The establishment of the Christian church is based on the claim that the revelation in Jesus as the Christ and as the perfect embodiment of the New Being is the final revelation.[11]

5. Faith and Reason

The reception of God as manifested in the New Being is done in faith and in faith alone. Yet it does not exclude the place and function of reason in its process. Rather, it is crucially important for man to employ fully the rational power he finds in himself in order to accomplish the descendency of theonomy most effectively. Tillich stated that by reaching the very depth of an autonomous reason, a theonomous state is being created.[12] Man must by all means make himself obeisant to the logos, the universal reason, which is immanent in mind and reality. He must obey its forms, structures, and laws with volitional willingness in order to bring about a theonomous state in his being and his reason. One of Tillich's self-imposed lifelong tasks as a philosophical theologian was to facilitate the realization of the fundamental unity

---

[10] Page 29.
[11] Pages 22f.
[12] Page 35.

between what Tillich termed a "receiving knowledge"[13] through faith and a "controlling knowledge"[14] by the act of reason and objective analysis. It is to prove the mutual immanence and basic unity of faith and reason, revelation and knowledge, theology and philosophy, and church and society. Tillich bluntly stated that the unity of theology with its theonomous reason and philosophy with its autonomous reason is a state of theonomy.[15] This analysis offers thereby a direction and a means of progress toward the harmony between religion and science, Christian education and secular education.

6. Culture

The intimacy of the relation between theonomy and culture, and the deepest degree of their mutual interpenetration, is indicated in Tillich's now famous aphorism: Religion is the substance of culture and culture the form of religion. Throughout his long life, Tillich passionately endeavored to awaken his students, followers, audiences, and readers to the realization that the new theonomy at hand should be established not only in religious spheres but also in every phase of cultural creation and expression. In fact, it cannot be done otherwise. This is so because religion and culture are one and the same on their profoundest level. Their relation will be proved further in conjunction with the findings in Section C, following, on the unity of religious and secular spheres.[16]

7. Kairos and History

When one is grasped by the powers of theonomy, he is in contact with a suprahistorical reality. In that ecstatic moment he is taken into the dynamic advent of the eternal in and through temporality. It is God's providential timing which makes a person, an institution, an event, or even an age, fulfilled, and which relates it to the unconditional. In that kairos moment, everyone and everything has only one direction, i.e., a vertical line reaching toward God. Theonomy thus elevates a piece out of the ordinary context of temporal things and events and makes it translucent for the Divine glory. In that instant something ultimate, infinite, and eternal happens in history, transforming and dedi-

---

[13] ST III, pp. 98-100 and 129-131.
[14] Ibid., pp. 97-100 and 102-105.
[15] Pages 41f.
[16] Pages 106-108.

cating it to the Divine. The eternal in this way participates in the moments of time, judging yet simultaneously elevating them to the eternal.

Tillich concluded that history comes from and moves toward periods of theonomy and that theonomy unites the absolute and the relative element in the interpretation of history. In this way and from this perspective, theonomy is inseparably related to human history. It is, in Tillich's words, the substance and meaning of history and a key to the theonomous interpretation of history.[17]

C. The Unity of Religious and Secular Spheres

1. Religion and Culture

The essential unity of religion and culture in Tillich's teaching is seen in his statement that "theonomy has been defined as a culture in which the ultimate meaning of existence shines through all finite forms of thoughts and action; the culture is transparent, and its creations are vessels of a spiritual content."[18] It is a state in which all the cultural forms and their autonomous creation, in art, in music, in sciences, in politics, in morals, in social relations, everywhere, all these forms have one point which has the line of the vertical. On another occasion Tillich said that in theonomy some ultimate meaning is expressed in all of the cultural activities and creations; it is expressed in the forms of the daily life of all the cultural production.[19] One other mark of theonomy is that it inserts back into all cultural expressions their spiritual substance, the center of meaning, and their continuous reference to the ultimate.

In Tillich's renowned aphorism—religion is the substance of culture and culture the form of religion—and from the foregoing quoted statements, it is evident that Tillich conceived religion as the principle which gives ultimate meaning to all cultural forms, or as the ultimate concern underlying every creative culture. There is no creative activity which can be performed apart from the creative ground of being, he insisted. This means that there is no cultural work completely excluded from religion, in the broader sense of the word. Religion is the substance or ground from which culture is nourished.

It is clear from the preceding summary paragraphs that, for Tillich,

---

[17] Pages 27f.
[18] Page 16.
[19] Pages 17f.

religion is related to culture in the depth of profundity. Without its religious substance, culture is left with an increasingly empty form, and with it culture receives meaning, seriousness, and depth and creates out of its own material a religious culture of its own—a theonomous culture in which may be found forms of both religious and secular culture with innumerable transitions between them.[20]

2. Theology and Other Disciplines

Tillich expressed as early as 1920s his personal preference to be identified as the man who had invented and held the position of "Belief-ful Realism" which he defined as "an attitude in which the reference to the transcendent and eternal source of meaning and ground of being is present." It is, furthermore, "the unconditional acceptance of the serious importance of our concrete situation in time and of the situation of time in general in the presence of eternity."[21] It is the free devotion of finite forms to the eternal and a state of being in which man goes beyond himself in order to return to himself in a new dimension.

Tillich contended that the impact of theonomy is not bound in any way to the religious realm but can even be effective through outspoken foes of religion and Christianity. This is so because at a theonomous moment, the Spiritual Presence speaks to all individuals, groups, and institutions, "grasping them, inspiring them, and transforming them."[22]

Based on this broad interpretation of the works of the Spiritual Presence, Tillich urged the theologians of all faiths to come out of their secluded theological "ivory towers" to start having a living dialogue with the so-called secular world.

More specifically, Tillich sounded a call to his fellow theologians to come out of their theological circles to have a dialogue with other disciplines such as political science, philosophy, medicine, particularly psychotherapy and psychiatry, art, and sociology. Theology must recognize the interdependence among all the fields of the human life process. In Tillich's mind, not only theological problems, but also sociological problems, psychological problems, problems of modern art, and problems of modern science are involved in the question of ultimate concern.[23] A theology which does not deal seriously with the criticism of religion by secular thought and some particular forms of secular faith, such as

---

[20] Pages 25f.
[21] Page 16.
[22] Page 19.
[23] Page 24.

liberalism, nationalism, and socialism, would be 'a-kairos'—missing the demand of the historical moment.

Tillich concluded that to anyone who is arrested by God in a theonomous moment the transcendence over religion, non-religion, or even anti-religion, is achieved and the unity of religion and the secular spheres is consummated.

D. More Similarities Than Differences in the Pedagogical Principles of Three Theologically Distinctive Groups in Christian Education

Through detailed analysis and careful comparison of the data presented in Chapters V, VI, and the first two parts in VII, it is the finding of this investigator that the differences found among the conservative, liberal, and reconstructed liberal groups in Christian education are more in terms of their theological convictions than in the underlying principles in pedagogy or in the actual teaching methods adhered to.

There are certain characteristics which are unique in each group and which are not shared by the other two groups. For example, the insistence of the conservatives that the center and foundation of a conservative Christian education is bi-polar, that is, it is rooted squarely on the sovereignty of Christ and the inerrant authority of the Holy Scriptures, is unique as far as its bi-polarity is concerned. The other two groups, particularly the reconstructed liberal group, also emphasize the important roles the doctrine of Christology and the Bible occupy in the content of their teaching but they never express these roles in terms of bi-polarity as the conservatives do. Another example is that the liberals and the reconstructed liberals do not stress the point of "faith over reason, divine enlightenment over human search"[24] as strongly and distinctively as conservatives do. In fact, the liberals do not stress it at all. Not only do the liberals not stress this point, but it is one of their unique characteristics to disagree with the conservatives on this score.[25]

The liberals maintain that man's rational power and search should have primacy over the so-called revealed truths accepted in faith. Anthropology is the heart of their system and the scientific, objective, and empirical approach constitutes a prevailing factor in their pedagogical principles. By adopting a pupil-centered approach in their teaching-learning enterprise, all three groups in Christian education covertly re-

---

[24] See page 97.
[25] Page 98, B, Number 1.

veal their adherence to the essentiality of the role freedom must play, particularly on the pupil's part. However, the liberals distinguish themselves by the very strong emphasis on the freedom that must be granted to and exercised by both the teacher and the pupils during their educational give-and-take in or outside of a classroom.

Another distinctive mark in the liberals' theory of Christian education is their emphasis on the social aspect in the educational enterprises. Being aware of the organic bonds that tie the members together in their respective groups within the Christian church, both conservatives and reconstructed liberals also adhere to, consciously or unconsciously, the necessity of educating their pupils in the social aspect of their fellowship and outreach. But they present this point neither as strongly nor as clearly as their liberal counterparts in the field of Christian education.

Over against the unique characteristics in theology and pedagogical principles of the conservatives and the liberals mentioned above, the reconstructed liberals are unique in their insistence on the point of relevance in their pedagogical principles as well as in their attitude toward divergent theories and practices. This means such things as relevance of content to method, teacher to pupil, theory to practice, ideals to possibilities. As was pointed out earlier,[26] one of the marks that distinguishes the reconstructed liberals from the other two groups in Christendom is their inclination toward synthesizing the divergent or even conflicting trends and qualities in various groups. They stress both the revealed character of the Christian faith and the place of reason in receiving, interpreting, and communicating the substance of the Christian message. But as said above, they do not see a bi-polarity here.

The reconstructed liberals also endeavor to maintain the balance between the transcendental and immanental qualities of God in their theology as well as in their pedagogical principles. They refuse to identify as some liberals do the Kingdom of God with human reformations and social institutions. Yet they teach that the Kingdom of God is God's reigning in human hearts, wills, and relationships. In summary, the reconstructed liberals are those Christians who strive to maintain a reasonable balance by simultaneously preserving the strengths and rejecting the weakness of various ecclesiastical and theological groups in the Christian church, on the basis of their own theological principles.

It must be noted from the paragraphs in the preceding four pages that the differences cited are mostly theological rather than pedagogical.

---

[26] Pages 60-62.

In sharp contrast to the small number of very important pedagogical differences discovered among the three distinctive groups in Christian education, it is the finding of this investigator that the similarities in the pedagogical principles and teaching methods among these three groups greatly outnumber their differences. This is attested by the lists of the characteristics of the pedagogical principles mutually shared by the conservative and liberal groups,[27] the conservative and reconstructed liberal groups,[28] and the liberal and reconstructed liberal groups.[29] These lists alone amply prove the point that there are numerous pedagogical principles that the three groups in Christian education commonly share together. The proof of this point is further reinforced by the list of the characteristics of the pedagogical principles shared by all three groups.[30]

It is seen in this list that there are altogether seven principles that are shared by all three groups in Christian education. Briefly, they are: (1) The teaching methods in Christian education are creative and flexible, (2) An imposition, authoritarian, or rote method is rejected, (3) An experience and pupil-centered approach is adhered to, (4) The role of reason is stressed, (5) Balance between content and experience is maintained, (6) A variety of methods is most desirable, and (7) The insights and findings of other fields of learning are accepted and utilized.

This researcher must conclude, therefore, that aside from the effects of certain differences in theological conviction and expression, there is no significant discrepancy or any sharp contrast in most of the pedagogical principles adhered to, and the teaching methods practiced, by the spokesmen among the conservative, liberal, and reconstructed liberal groups in the Protestant Christian education.

E. The Second Hypothesis Is Sustained

In spite of the foregoing finding, this researcher concludes that the second hypothesis in this thesis must be sustained: that the concept of theonomy in Tillich is most compatible with the pedagogical principles of the reconstructed liberal group, his concept of heteronomy with the pedagogical principles of the conservative group, and his concept of autonomy with those of the liberal group.

---

[27] Page 99.
[28] Pages 99f.
[29] Page 100.
[30] Pages 100f.

110

This conclusion is reached on the basis of the study and comparison of (1) the concepts of theonomy, autonomy, and heteronomy in Tillich's thought as found in Chapters III and IV, (2) the pedagogical principles of the conservative, liberal, and reconstructed liberal groups in Protestant Christian education in Chapters V and VI, and (3) the summary and conclusion in the present chapter, VII, parts I, II, and III, A through D. The study reveals that although there are numerous similarities found in the pedagogical principles adhered to by the representatives of the three distinctive groups in Christian education, the profound differences in their basic theological assumptions and convictions overshadow their pedagogical similarities. The pedagogical principles of the conservative, liberal, and reconstructed liberal groups cannot but reflect the fundamental theological tenets on which their educational theory and practice are based. The few variations are therefore extremely important.

For example, though sharing many characteristics in actual teaching methods with liberals and reconstructed liberals the conservatives are still those who believe in and hold strong allegiance to the basic truths of Scriptures and who firmly believe in the articles of faith, the most conspicuous of which is the authority and infallibility of the Bible. They are those who volitionally and willingly submit themselves to the authority of the Scriptures, and in a lesser degree, to the rule of certain creeds, articles of faith, doctrinal statements, or strict standards of conduct.[31]

Even when they are discussing explicitly the pedagogical principles in Christian education, the conservatives maintain that the religious educators' task is to discover God's teaching methods through the inspiration and assistance of the Holy Spirit, and that belief is the key to this enterprise. In other words, in order to discover God's ways of teaching one must believe in and commit oneself wholly to God, Jesus Christ, the work of the Holy Spirit, and the truths contained in the Holy Scriptures. Faith over reason, divine enlightenment over human search, is the key to the conservatives' pedagogical principles.[32]

These basic theological convictions and pedagogical assumptions among conservatives are most compatible with the teachings on heteronomy in Tillich's theological system.

In sharp contrast with the heteronomous tendencies found among the conservative religious educators, the liberals are those who believe

---

[31] Pages 58f.
[32] Page 97.

in the infinite dignity and value of man as man and who uphold anthropology as the heart of their system. They believe in the use of the scientific method of inquiry, and of historical and textual criticisms in the study of the Scriptures, and they adhere to freedom from prior commitments and to the willingness to break through present structures of thought or practice in order to formulate new patterns.

The method most acceptable to the liberals is that of critical inquiry: the logical processes of whatever sort by which anything—any law, any common belief, any experience—may be explored in the quest for knowledge or in the exposing of old falsehoods. Naturally they reject categorically the old views of authority, Scriptural or otherwise, building their doctrines and beliefs on religious experience and on rational-empirical grounds. With their particular anthropologic orientation, the liberals of course strongly emphasize the place of the freedom that must be granted to and exercised by teachers and students alike in their theological and educational enterprises. Moreover, being scientific, or at least critically inquiring, in their approach to any problem or experience, the liberals believe in being objective and rational in their basic assumptions. They believe that man's rational power and search should have primacy over the so-called revealed truths accepted in faith.[33]

In conclusion, an anthropocentric, independent, scientific, objective, and empirical approach to any problem or any task constitutes for liberals a prevailing factor in their pedagogical principles and this spirit and attitude is very compatible with the teachings on the concept of autonomy in Tillich's theology, although one must not forget that autonomy for him includes other things than the critical, inquiring approach. It includes the idea of existential freedom, for instance.

Over against the conservatives and liberals, the reconstructed liberals are those who stress both the revealed character of the Christian faith and the place of reason in determining the substance of Christian belief. They insist that rational faculties in man must be fully utilized "to receive revelation, to distinguish between true and false revelation claims, and to interpret the implications of revelation for living and to establish bridges of understanding for communication of the revealed truth to many kinds of people."[34]

The reconstructed liberals, although emphasizing more than the majority of the liberals do the uniqueness of the Christian message

---

[33] Page 108.
[34] Page 60.

112

and the vital importance of the Holy Scriptures, nonetheless insist that God has also disclosed himself and much truth among men of other races, traditions, and religions.[35] They maintain a balance between God's transcendent and immanent nature and teach that the Kingdom of God is not identical with human accomplishments of reform or with certain social institutions. They insist that the Kingdom of God is God's reigning in human hearts, wills, and relationships. "Its coming depends on God, but also upon the faithful obedience of man in subjecting all human experience, institutions, and relationships to his rule."[36]

In summary, the reconstructed liberals are those who endeavor to maintain a reasonable balance by simultaneously preserving the strengths and rejecting the weaknesses of both conservative and liberal groups. They are quite open to all scientific findings but make a sharp distinction between Christian faith and the prevailing spirit of modern culture. Their inclination toward synthesizing the divergent or even conflicting trends and qualities in various groups reminds the readers of Tillich's teachings on theonomy as the ground from which both autonomy and heteronomy stem. It must be concluded therefore that the spirit of the reconstructed liberal group is highly compatible with the concept of theonomy in Tillich's thought.

Based on the above summary paragraphs, the second hypothesis in this thesis is sustained.

F.   TILLICH ON EDUCATION

Although it is not the purpose of this thesis to discover and interpret Tillich's own statements on education, it is interesting to know that Tillich has commented on education since as early as the 1920s. Another research student would find a mine of materials on education in Tillich—although he never wrote systematically or at length on the subject.

The present thesis will end with a very few of Tillich's statements on education.

In 1932, in The Religious Situation, he wrote that "every type of education is ultimately dependent upon the spiritual meaning which determines what its goals and methods are to be,"[37] and "every educa-

---

[35] Note: This is one of the major points in Tillich's Christianity and the Encounter of the World Religions and a posthumous volume, The Future of Religions.

[36] Page 61.

[37] The Religious Situation, p. 146.

tional method which does not rest upon a common relationship of both teacher and taught to something ultimate, to the eternal, is inadequate."[38] This is so because for him in the sphere of the finite every goal that is set up, every method which is employed, is doubtful, limited, and ultimately irresponsible.

> Only the Unconditioned can create unconditioned responsibility and therewith a relationship of teacher and taught which rests upon mutual responsibility and the possibility of unqualified loyalty. Given this common basis, the technique of communicating forms, which is the real problem of scientific pedagogy, becomes a question of the second order.[39]

Writing in the same book on some of the reform movements such as the one promoted in Germany by the League of School Reformers, Tillich regarded them as a passionate reaction against and attack upon capitalist education. He expressed the ideals of these reformers as follows:

> The authoritative communication of the subject matter is opposed; originality and creative activity on the part of the pupil are encouraged. Vital participation of the pupil in perceptual reality is to take the place of the intellectual communication of the rational and abstract form of things. Fellowship between the pupils and between them and the teacher is proclaimed as the ideal form of the educational relationship.[40]

Tillich saw that these principles were of greatest importance for the religious situation of that day and particularly of the future. Yet, the fundamental presupposition for the realization of all these demands was present only in desire and not in fact. What was missing was a "holy" meaning for the educational ideal and method. As long as this is missing, and to the extent to which it is missing, anti-capitalist pedagogy will be in a difficult position and will remain more a signpost toward the future than a creative force in the present. What is genuinely needed is a combination of realism and faith, that is, Belief-ful Realism.[41] This term, Belief-ful Realism, contained the essentials of the ideas later contained in the term theonomy.

Having achieved his own autonomous freedom after experiencing a

---

[38] *Ibid.*, pp. 146f.
[39] *Ibid.*, p. 147.
[40] *Ibid.*, p. 149.
[41] *Ibid.*, pp. 149f.

painful break-through from his father's authoritarian attitude,[42] Tillich was naturally opposed to an authoritarian method in teaching. He also rejected the pedagogical attitude of what he called a "complete self-restriction" on the educator's part as exemplified in some types of progressive schools.[43] What he adhered to as far as educational aim is concerned is something that all three groups in Christian education dealt with in this thesis will undoubtedly endorse. He said that under the impact of the Spiritual Presence the educational act creates "theonomy in the centered person by directing him toward the ultimate from which he receives independence without internal chaos." "If the educational or guiding communion between person and person is raised beyond itself by the Spiritual Presence," he continued, "the split between subject and object in both relations is fragmentarily conquered and humanity is fragmentarily achieved."[44]

The following are some of the quotations from Tillich which are presented to the readers without interpretation or explanation.

> The theonomous word for education is "initiation." While the word "education" points to the terminus a quo, the "where from," the word "initiation" points to the terminus ad quem, the "where to."[45]

Speaking on the topic of "Theology of Education," at St. Paul's School in Concord, New Hampshire, in 1957, Tillich had this to say:

> The inducting education of the Church School can and must include the principle of humanist education, the correlation between question and answer . . . the opening up of all human possibilities, and the providing for chances which the pupil may develop in freedom.[46]

Elaborating on the point of correlation, or relevance, Tillich cited the following as one of the main difficulties in Christian education:

> Religious induction . . . has to give answers to questions which never have been asked by the child. In speaking of God and the Christ and the Church, or of sin and salvation and the kingdom of God, religious education mediates a material which cannot be

---

[42] See page 9 of this thesis.
[43] See ST III, pp. 260f.
[44] Ibid., p. 261.
[45] The Protestant Era, p. 65.
[46] See "Theology of Education," The Church School in Our Time, 1957, p. 12.

received by the mind of those who have not asked the questions to which these words give answers.[47]

The following quotation shows that the principles of content-plus-experience, of participation, and of gradation according to the pupil's level of maturity are all implicitly embraced by Tillich himself. Writing specifically on the educational function of the church, he said:

> The church's task is to introduce each new generation into the reality of the Spiritual Community, into its faith and into its love. This happens through participation in degrees of maturity, and it happens through interpretation in degrees of understanding. There is no understanding of a church's life without participation; but without understanding the participation becomes mechanical and compulsory.[48]

[47] *Theology of Culture*, p. 154.
[48] *ST III*, p. 194. See also *The Religious Situation*, p. 149.

Selected Bibliography

PART I.   THEOLOGY

A.   Books

Adams, James L. *Paul Tillich's Philosophy of Culture, Science, and Religion.* New York: Harper and Row, Publishers, 1965.

Athanasius, St. *The Incarnation of the Word of God.* New York: The Macmillan Company. Seventh printing, 1959.

Aulen, Gustaf. *The Faith of the Christian Church.* Philadelphia: The Muhlenberg Press. Eighth printing, 1948.

————. *Christus Victor.* New York: The Macmillan Company. Sixth printing, 1960.

Barth, Karl. *The Word of God and the Word of Man.* New York: Harper and Brothers, 1957.

————. *The Faith of Our Church.* New York: Meridian Books, Inc., 1958.

————. *Dogmatics in Outline.* New York: Harper and Brothers, 1959.

Brown, D. Mackenzie. *Ultimate Concern: Tillich in Dialogue.* New York: Harper and Row, Publishers, 1965.

Brunner, Emil. *Revelation and Reason.* Philadelphia: The Westminster Press, 1946.

Calvin, John. *Institutes of the Christian Religion.* 2 volumes. Grand Rapids, Michigan: William B. Eerdmans Publishing Company, 1957.

Cooper, John C. *The Roots of the Radical Theology.* Philadelphia: The Westminster Press, 1967.

Crawford, W. Rex (ed.). *The Cultural Migration.* Philadelphia: The University of Pennsylvania Press, 1953.

DeWolf, L. Harold. *A Theology of the Living Church.* New York: Harper and Brothers. Revised edition, 1960.

Farley, Edward. *The Transcendence of God.* Philadelphia: The Westminster Press, 1960.

117

Feuerbach, Ludwig. *The Essence of Christianity*. New York: Harper and Brothers, 1957.

Halverson, Marvin (ed.). *Handbook of Christian Theology*. New York: Meridian Books, Inc., 1958.

Hamilton, Kenneth. *The System and the Gospel*. New York: The Macmillan Company, 1963.

Hammond, Guyton B. *The Power of Transcendence*. St. Louis, Missouri: The Bethany Press, 1966.

Herberg, Will (ed.). *Four Existentialist Theologians*. Garden City: Doubleday and Company, Inc., 1958.

Huxley, Julian. *Religion without Revelation*. New York: Mentor Books, 1958.

Jaspers, Karl. *Man in the Modern Age*. Garden City: Doubleday and Company, Inc., 1957.

Kierkegaard, Soren. *Fear and Trembling/The Sickness Unto Death*. New York: Doubleday and Company, Inc., 1954.

————. *Purity of Heart Is to Will One Thing*. New York: Harper and Brothers, 1956.

Kraemer, Hendrik. *Religion and the Christian Faith*. London: Lutterworth Press, 1956.

Landon, Harold R. (ed.). *Reinhold Niebuhr: A Prophetic Voice in Our Time*. Greenwich, Connecticut: The Seabury Press, 1962.

Leibrecht, Walter (ed.). *Religion and Culture: Essays in Honor of Paul Tillich*. New York: Harper and Brothers, 1959.

Macquarrie, John. *An Existentialist Theology*. London: SCM Press Ltd., 1955.

McKelway, Alexander J. *The Systematic Theology of Paul Tillich*. Richmond, Virginia: John Knox Press, 1964.

Martin, Bernard. *The Existentialist Theology of Paul Tillich*. New York: Bookman Associates Inc., 1963.

Niebuhr, H. Richard. *Christ and Culture*. New York: Harper and Brothers, 1951.

Otto, Rudolf. *The Idea of the Holy*. New York: Oxford University Press. Fifth Galaxy printing, 1963.

Reinisch, Leonhard (ed.). *Theologians of Our Time*. Notre Dame, Indiana: The University of Notre Dame Press, 1964.

Smith, Huston (ed.). *The Search for America*. Englewood Cliffs, New Jersey: Prentice-Hall, Inc., 1959.

Souter, Alexander. *A Pocket Lexicon to the Greek New Testament*. New York: Oxford University Press, 1948.

Tavard, George H. *Paul Tillich and the Christian Message*. New York: Charles Scribner's Sons, 1962.

Thielicke, Helmut. *Christ and the Meaning of Life*. New York: Harper and Row, 1962.

Thomas, J. Heywood. *Paul Tillich: An Appraisal*. Philadelphia: The Westminster Press, 1963.

————. *Paul Tillich*. Richmond, Virginia: John Knox Press, 1966.

Tillich, Paul. *The Religious Situation*. New York: Henry Holt and Company, 1932. Meridian Books, 1959.

————. *The Interpretation of History*. New York: Charles Scribner's Sons, 1936.

————. *The Protestant Era*. Chicago: The University of Chicago Press, 1948.

————. *The Shaking of the Foundations*. New York: Charles Scribner's Sons, 1948.

————. *Systematic Theology I*. Chicago: The University of Chicago Press, 1951.

————. *The Courage to Be*. New Haven: Yale University Press, 1952.

————. *Love, Power, and Justice*. New York: Oxford University Press, 1954.

————. *The New Being*. New York: Charles Scribner's Sons, 1955.

————. *Biblical Religion and the Search for Ultimate Reality*. Chicago: The University of Chicago Press, 1955.

————. *Systematic Theology II*. Chicago: The University of Chicago Press, 1957.

————. *Dynamics of Faith*. New York: Harper Torchbooks, 1957.

————. *Theology of Culture*. New York: Oxford University Press, 1959.

————. *Systematic Theology III*. Chicago: The University of Chicago Press, 1963.

————. *Morality and Beyond*. New York: Harper and Row, Publishers, 1963.

————. *Eternal Now*. New York: Charles Scribner's Sons, 1963.

————. *Christianity and the Encounter of World Religions*. New York: Columbia University Press, 1963.

————. *The World Situation*. Philadelphia: Fortress Press, 1965.

————. *The Future of Religions*. New York: Harper and Row, Publishers, 1966.

————. *Perspectives on 19th and 20th Century Protestant Theology*. New York: Harper and Row, Publishers, 1967.

————. *My Search for Absolutes*. New York: Simon and Schuster, Inc., 1967.

Van Dusen, Henry (ed.). *The Christian Answer*. New York: Charles Scribner's Sons, 1945.

Vogt, Von Ogden. *Art and Religion*. New Haven: Yale University Press, 1921.

Weber, Max. *The Protestant Ethics and the Spirit of Capitalism*. New York: Charles Scribner's Sons, 1958.

Williams, Daniel D. *What Present Day Theologians Are Thinking.* New York: Harper and Brothers. Revised edition, 1959.

B. Published Lectures

Tillich, Paul. "The Recovery of the Prophetic Tradition in the Reformation." Three lectures delivered at the Washington Cathedral Library, Washington, D.C., November-December, 1950.

————. "A History of Christian Thought." Lectures at Union Theological Seminary, New York, Spring Semester, 1953.

————. "Theology of Education," *The Church School in Our Time.* Address at St. Paul's School, Concord, N. H., 1957, pp. 3-14.

————. "The Idea of God as Affected by Modern Knowledge." Lecture delivered at Unitarian Church, Lancaster, Pennsylvania, November, 1957.

————. "Philosophical Background of My Theology." Lecture at St. Paul's University, Tokyo, Japan, May 2, 1960.

C. Unpublished Dissertations

Jackson, Harold. "The Significance of Paul Tillich's Theology for a Philosophy of Religious Education." Unpublished Ed.D. dissertation, Stanford University, California, 1956.

Song, Choan-seng. "The Relation of Divine Revelation and Man's Religion in the Theologies of Karl Barth and Paul Tillich." Unpublished Th.D. dissertation, Union Theological Seminary, New York, 1964.

D. Periodicals

Allen, George and Unwin. "Review: Dynamics of Faith," *Scottish Journal of Theology,* June, 1958, pp. 200- 202.

Baillie, John. "Review: Systematic Theology I," *Theology Today,* January, 1952, pp. 566-568.

Clarke, Bowman L. "God and the Symbolic in Tillich," *Anglican Theological Review,* July, 1961, pp. 302-311.

Fern, Deane W. "Conflicting Trends in Protestant Thinking," *Religion in Life,* Winter, 1955, pp. 582-594.

Furuya, Yasuo Carl. "Apologetic or Kerygmatic Theology," *Theology Today,* January, 1960, pp. 471-480.

Gernest, A. C. "Review: Biblical Religion and the Search for Ultimate Reality," *Encounter,* Spring, 1956, pp. 177-180.

Gealy, Frederic D. "Review: The New Being," *Perkins School of Theology Journal,* Winter, 1956, pp. 30-31.

Grant, Frederic C. "Editorial: Paul Tillich," *Anglican Theological Review*, July, 1961, pp. 241-244.

Greene, Theodore. "Review: Love, Power, and Justice," *Theology Today*, October, 1955, pp. 388-391.

Harvard Divinity Bulletin. "Words for Paul Tillich," January, 1966, pp. 1-28.

Hartshorne, Charles. "Tillich and the Other Great Traditions," *Anglican Theological Review*, July, 1961, pp. 245-259.

Herberg, Will. "Reinhold Niebuhr and Paul Tillich: Two Ways in American Protestant Theology," *Chaplain*, October, 1959, pp. 3-9 and 36.

Hopper, David H. "Toward Understanding the Thought of Paul Tillich," *The Princeton Seminary Bulletin*, April, 1962, pp. 36-43.

Housley, John B. "Paul Tillich and Christian Education," *Religious Education*, July-August, 1967, pp. 307-315.

Hunter, Howard E. "Tillich and Tennant: Two Types of Philosophical Theology," *Crane Review*, Spring, 1959, pp. 100-110.

Livergood, Norman. "A Critique of Tillich's Theology," *Crane Review*, Spring, 1962, pp. 153-163.

McCord, James I. "Review: Love, Power, and Justice," *Interpretation*, April, 1955, pp. 221-222.

MacKirachan, J. Frederick. "The Preaching of Paul Tillich," *The Princeton Seminary Bulletin*, January, 1960, pp. 33-42.

New York Times. "The Mind and the Heart," October 17, 1955, p. 54.

————. "A Theology for Protestants," March 16, 1959, pp. 46-52.

Niebuhr, Reinhold. "The Contribution of Paul Tillich," *Religion in Life*, Autumn Number, 1937, pp. 574-581.

Pittenger, W. Norman. "Paul Tillich as a Theologian: An Appreciation," *Anglican Theological Review*, July, 1961, pp. 268-286.

Rose, Delbert R. "Paul Tillich: An Existential Theologian," *Asbury Seminarian*, Summer, 1957, pp. 15-20.

Skinner, John E. "A Critique of Tillich's Ontology," *Anglican Theological Review*, January, 1957, pp. 53-61.

Stiernotte, Alfred P. "Paul Tillich—Mystic, Rationalist, Universalist," *Crane Review*, Spring, 1962, pp. 164-180.

Tillich, Paul. "The Religious Situation in Germany Today," *Religion in Life*, Spring, 1934, pp. 163-173.

————. "What Is Wrong with the 'Dialectic' Theology?" *The Journal of Religion*, April, 1935, pp. 127-145.

————. "The End of the Protestant Era," *The Student World*, First Quarter, 1937, pp. 1-5.

————. "The Significance of the Historical Jesus for the Christian Faith," *Monday Forum Talks*, Union Theological Seminary, New York, February 28, 1938, pp. 1-4.

————. "The Attack of Dialectical Materialism on Christianity," *The Student World*, Second Quarter, 1938, pp. 115-125.

————. "War Aims," *Protestant*, January 16, 1942, pp. 1-19.

————. "Trends in Religious Thought That Affect Social Outlook," *Religion and the World Order*, 1943, pp. 17-28.

————. "The God of History," *Christianity and Crisis*, May 1, 1944, pp. 5-6.

————. "Now Concerning Spiritual Gifts," *Union Review*, December, 1944, pp. 15-17.

————. "Conscience in Western Thought and the Idea of a Transmoral Conscience," *Crozer Quarterly*, October, 1945, pp. 289-300.

————. "A Reinterpretation of the Doctrine of the Incarnation," *Church Quarterly Review*, London, January-March, 1949, pp. 133-148.

————. "Beyond Religious Socialism," *The Christian Century*, June 15, 1949, pp. 732-733.

————. "The Present Theological Situation in the Light of the Continental European Development," *Theology Today*, October, 1949, pp. 299-310.

————. "Religion and Intellectuals," *Partisan Review*, March, 1950, pp. 254-256.

————. "The Protestant Vision," *Chicago Theological Seminary Register*, March, 1950, pp. 8-12.

————. "Victory in Defeat: The Meaning of History in the Light of Christian Prophetism," *Interpretation*, January, 1952, pp. 17-26.

————. "Christian Criteria for Our Culture," *Criterion*, October, 1952, pp. 1 and 3-4.

————. "Karen Horney: A Funeral Address," *Pastoral Psychology*, May, 1953, pp. 11-13 and 66.

————. "Jewish Influences on Contemporary Christian Theology," *Cross Currents*, Spring, 1953, pp. 35-42.

————. "Being and Love," *Pastoral Psychology*, April, 1954, pp. 43-48.

————. "Religion and Its Intellectual Critics," *Christianity and Crisis*, March 7, 1955, pp. 19-22.

————. "The Theology of Missions," *Christianity and Crisis*, April 4, 1955, pp. 35-38.

————. "What Is Truth?" *Canadian Journal of Theology*, July, 1955, pp. 117-122.

————. "Erich Fromm's 'The Sane Society'," *Pastoral Psychology*, September, 1955, pp. 13-16.

————. "Where Do We Go from Here in Theology?" *Religion in Life*, Winter, 1955-1956, pp. 19-21.

————. "Heal the Sick; Cast Out the Demons," *Religious Education*, November-December, 1955, pp. 379-382.

————. "Theology and Counseling," *Journal of Pastoral Care*, Winter, 1956, pp. 193-200.

————. "God's Pursuit of Man," *Bangor Alumni Bulletin*, April, 1958, pp. 21-25.

————. "Beyond the Usual Alternative," *The Christian Century*, May 7, 1958, pp. 553-555.

————. "Psychoanalysis, Existentialism, and Theology," *Pastoral Psychology*, October, 1958, pp. 9-17.

————. "Art and Ultimate Reality," *Cross Currents*, February 17, 1959, pp. 1-14.

————. "Beyond Utopianism and Escape from History," *Colgate-Rochester Divinity School Bulletin*, May, 1959, pp. 32-40.

————. "Religion and the Ethical Norms," *VOX*, Summer, 1959, pp. 4-12.

————. "Dimensions, Levels, and the Unity of Life," *Kenyon Alumni Bulletin*, October-December, 1959, pp. 4-8.

————. "The Impact of Pastoral Psychology on Theological Thought," *Pastoral Psychology*, February, 1960, pp. 17-23.

————. "The Divine Name," *Christianity and Crisis*, May 2, 1960, pp. 55-58.

————. "The Basic Ideas of Religious Socialism," *International House of Japan, Inc. Bulletin*, 1960, pp. 11-15 and 32.

————. "Mission: A Basic Element in the Life of the Church," *United Church Herald*, June 15, 1961, pp. 20-21.

————. "Man, the Earth and the Universe," *Christianity and Crisis*, June 25, 1962, pp. 108-112.

————. "Question on Brunner's Epistemology," *The Christian Century*, October 24, 1962, pp. 1284-1287.

————. "The Riddle of Inequality," *United Church Herald*, September 19, 1963, pp. 12-14.

————. "Creative Love in Education," *World Christian Education*, Third Quarter, 1963, pp. 70 and 75.

————. "Salvation: Baccalaureate Address," *The Princeton Seminary Bulletin*, October, 1963, pp. 4-9.

————. "In Thinking Be Mature," *Pulpit*, November, 1963, pp. 4-6.

————. "Philosophy of Social Work," *Pastoral Psychology*, December, 1963, pp. 27-30 and 65.

————. "The Basis of Genuine Hope for Peace on Earth," *Social Progress*, May-June, 1965, pp. 16-20.

Van Buren, Paul. "Review: Systematic Theology III," *The Christian Century*, February 5, 1964, pp. 177-179.

Wagner, Herndon. "Review: Biblical Religion and the Search for Ultimate Reality," *Perkins School of Theology Journal*, Winter, 1956, pp. 30-31.

Weigel, Gustave. "The Theological Significance of Paul Tillich," *Cross Currents*, Winter, 1956, pp. 141-155.

Young, Norman. "Some Implications in Tillich's Theology for Christian Education," *Religious Education*, May-June, 1965, pp. 230-237.

PART II.   CHRISTIAN EDUCATION

Bushnell, Horace. *Christian Nurture.* New Haven: Yale University Press, 1947.

Butler, J. Donald. *Four Philosophies and Their Practice in Education and Religion.* New York: Harper and Brothers, 1957.

Coe, George A. *A Social Theory of Religious Education.* New York: Charles Scribner's Sons, 1917.

————. *What Is Christian Education?* New York: Charles Scribner's Sons, 1929.

Cully, Kendig B. (ed.). *The Westminster Dictionary of Christian Education.* Philadelphia: The Westminster Press, 1963.

Cully, Iris V. *The Dynamics of Christian Education.* Philadelphia: The Westminster Press, 1958.

————. *Children in the Church.* Philadelphia: The Westminster Press, 1960.

Elliot, Harrison S. *Can Religious Education Be Christian?* New York: The Macmillan Company, 1940.

Fahs, Sophia L. *Today's Children and Yesterday's Heritage.* Boston: The Beacon Press, Inc., 1952.

Fallaw, Wesner. *Church Education for Tomorrow.* Philadelphia: The Westminster Press, 1960.

Henderlite, Rachel. *The Holy Spirit in Christian Education.* Philadelphia: The Westminster Press, 1964.

Howe, Reuel L. *Man's Need and God's Action.* Greenwich, Connecticut: Seabury Press. Sixth printing, 1957.

————. *The Miracle of Dialogue.* Greenwich, Connecticut: Seabury Press, 1963.

Horne, Herman H. *The Philosophy of Christian Education.* New York: Fleming H. Revell Company, 1937.

LeBar, Lois E. *Education That Is Christian.* Westwood, New Jersey: Fleming H. Revell Company, 1958.

Little, Lawrence. *Foundations for Philosophy of Christian Education.* Nashville: Abingdon Press, 1962.

Little, Sara. *Learning Together in the Christian Fellowship.* Richmond, Virginia: John Knox Press, 1962.

Miller, Randolph C. *The Clue to Christian Education.* New York: Charles Scribner's Sons, 1952.

————. *Education for Christian Living.* Englewood Cliffs: Prentice-Hall, Inc. Fifth printing, 1962.

Niebuhr, H. Richard and Williams, Daniel D. (ed.). *The Ministry in Historical Perspectives.* New York: Harper and Brothers, 1956.

Sherrill, Lewis J. *The Rise of Christian Education.* New York: The Macmillan Company, 1944.

————. *The Gift of Power.* New York: The Macmillan Company, 1955.

Schreyer, George M. *Christian Education in Theological Focus.* New York: United Church Press, 1962.

Smart, James D. *The Teaching Ministry of the Church.* Philadelphia: The Westminster Press, 1954.

Taylor, Marvin J. (ed.). *Religious Education.* Nashville: Abingdon Press, 1960.

VanDusen, Henry P. *God in Education.* New York: Charles Scribner's Sons, 1951.

Vieth, Paul H. (ed.). *The Church and Christian Education.* St. Louis: The Bethany Press, 1947.

Wyckoff, D. Campbell. *The Task of Christian Education.* Philadelphia: The Westminster Press, 1955.

————. *The Gospel and Christian Education.* Philadelphia: The Westminster Press, 1959.

PART III. EDUCATION AND OTHERS

Barzun, Jacques and Graff, Henry F. *The Modern Researcher.* New York: Harcourt, Brace and Company, 1957.

Brameld, Theodore. *Philosophies of Education in Cultural Perspective.* New York: Holt, Rinehart and Winston, 1955.

Broudy, Harry S. *Building a Philosophy of Education.* Englewood Cliffs: Prentice-Hall, Inc., 1955.

Cantor, Nathaniel F. *The Teaching-learning Process.* New York: The Dryden Press, 1954.

Dewey, John. *Democracy and Education.* New York: The Macmillan Company. Paperbooks edition, Second printing, 1963.

Frank, Eric. *Philosophical Understanding and Religious Truth.* Oxford: Oxford University Press. Sixth printing, 1959.

Gottschalk, Louis. *Understanding History*. New York: Alfred Knoff, Inc., 1958.

Horne, Herman H. *This New Education*. New York: Abingdon Press, 1931.

Phenix, Philip H. (ed.). *Philosophies of Education*. New York: John Wiley and Sons, Inc. Second printing, 1962.

Whitehead, Alfred N. *The Aims of Educaton*. New York: The Macmillan Company. Fifth printing, 1954.

Date Due			

Demco 38-297